W9-BBC-393

Questions and Answers about Fluency

Overview & Anticipation Guide   2

1. What Is Fluency?   3
2. Why Is Fluency Important?   3
3. Does Fluency Apply to Silent Reading?   4
4. How Is Rate of Reading Determined?   4
5. What Oral Reading Rates Are Appropriate for Different Grade Levels?   5
6. What Are Some Ways to Assess Fluency?   7
7. What's Wrong with Round Robin Oral Reading?   10
8. What Part of the Reading Program Should Be Devoted to Fluency Instruction?   14
9. What Insights from Fluency Can Be Drawn from Research and Expert Opinion?   15
10. What Factors Can Impact Fluency?   16
11. When Should Fluency Instruction Begin?   16
12. What Are the Basic Principles of Fluency Instruction?   16

___ OVERVIEW & ANTICIPATION GUIDE ___

This part of the book provides a series of questions and answers related to fluency. We have also provided an anticipation guide so you can react to some statements about fluency before you read the questions and answers.

___ Anticipation Guide ___ for Fluency

DIRECTIONS

Before reading the questions and answers, read the statements below and check those with which you agree.

BEFORE READING

Agree	Disagree	
_____	_____	1. Fluency in reading is most relevant at the beginning stages of reading.
_____	_____	2. Fluency is independent of comprehension.
_____	_____	3. Research has identified several methods to increase reading fluency.
_____	_____	4. Oral reading fluency is developed best through independent reading.
_____	_____	5. One aspect of fluency can be judged by determining the student's rate of reading in words per minute (WPM).
_____	_____	6. It is appropriate to consider fluency in silent reading.
_____	_____	7. Fluency is actually speed of reading.
_____	_____	8. Fluency strategies are primarily for students experiencing difficulty in reading.
_____	_____	9. Students should adjust reading rate according to their purposes for reading.
_____	_____	10. A reasonable oral fluency rate for third-grade students is 160 words per minute (WPM) by the end of the school year.
_____	_____	11. Round robin oral reading is an effective fluency activity.

Fluency

- *Questions*
  - *Answers*
    - *Evidence-Based Strategies*

Jerry L. Johns

Roberta L. Berglund

 KENDALL/HUNT PUBLISHING COMPANY
4050 Westmark Drive Dubuque, Iowa 52002

www.kendallhunt.com

Book Team

Chairman and Chief Executive Officer: Mark C. Falb
Vice President, Director of National Book Program: Alfred C. Grisanti
Editorial Development Supervisor: Georgia Botsford
Assistant Vice President, Production Services: Chris O'Brien
Production Services Manager: Kathy Hanson
Prepress Editor: Ellen Kaune
Design Manager: Jodi Splinter
Designer: Deb Howes

Author Information for Correspondence and Workshops

Jerry L. Johns, Ph.D.
Consultant in Reading
2105 Eastgate Drive
Sycamore, IL 60178
E-mail: *jjohns@niu.edu*
815-895-3022

Roberta L. Berglund, Ed.D.
Consultant in Reading/Language Arts
Two Oak Brook Club Drive
Suite C-102
Oak Brook, IL 60523
E-mail: *bberglund@rocketmail.com*
630-782-5852

Ordering Information

Address: Kendall/Hunt Publishing Company
4050 Westmark Drive, P.O. Box 1840
Dubuque, IA 52004-1840

Telephone: 800-247-3458, Ext. 5

Web site: www.kendallhunt.com

Fax: 800-772-9165

Copyright © 2002 by Kendall/Hunt Publishing Company

ISBN 0-7872-9143-9

Printed in the United States of America
10 9 8 7 6 5 4 3 2

Contents

Preface   iv
About the Authors   v

Part 1: Questions and Answers about Fluency   1

Overview & Anticipation Guide   2
1. What Is Fluency?   3
2. Why Is Fluency Important?   3
3. Does Fluency Apply to Silent Reading?   4
4. How Is Rate of Reading Determined?   4
5. What Oral Reading Rates Are Appropriate for Different Grade Levels?   5
6. What Are Some Ways to Assess Fluency?   7
7. What's Wrong with Round Robin Oral Reading?   10
8. What Part of the Reading Program Should Be Devoted to Fluency Instruction?   14
9. What Insights Can Be Drawn from Research and Expert Opinion?   15
10. What Factors Can Impact Fluency?   16
11. When Should Fluency Instruction Begin?   16
12. What Are the Basic Principles of Fluency Instruction?   16

Part 2: Evidence-Based Strategies, Activities, and Resources   19

Overview   20

Classroom Instruction   22
Basic Sight Words   23
Language Experience   27
Shared Book Experience   29
Echo Reading   31
Choral Reading   32
Antiphonal Reading   33
Readers Theater   35
Radio Reading   37
Oral Recitation Lesson   40
Fluency Development Lesson   42
Say It Like the Character   43
Super Signals   45
Phrase Boundaries   47

Assisted Reading   48
Paired Reading   49
Neurological Impress Method   52
Preview-Pause-Prompt-Praise   53
Structured Repeated Readings   56
Tape, Check, Chart   59
Reading While Listening   61

Independent Practice   65
Sustained Silent Reading (SSR)   66
Read and Relax   69

Appendices   73
Appendix A—Answers to Anticipation Guide for Fluency   75
Appendix B—Scripts for Readers Theater   77

References   87

Index   91

Preface

Fluency is an important consideration in all classroom reading programs. It is also a critical element in programs designed for readers who struggle. This compact, focused book will help you understand the major aspects of fluency. Part 1 presents a series of questions and answers about the basic principles of fluency. Part 2 contains evidence-based strategies, practical activities, and resources that will help you promote fluency. Our intention is to provide you with a solid basis for understanding fluency and to offer numerous ways to help students become confident readers who demonstrate greater fluency and automaticity.

The audience for this helpful book includes classroom teachers, prospective elementary teachers, reading specialists, and other professionals involved in schools and educational agencies. It is also a useful supplement for a wide variety of reading courses.

About the Authors

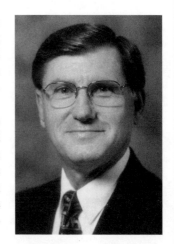

Jerry L. Johns, Distinguished Teaching Professor Emeritus of Northern Illinois University, is the 2002–2003 president of the International Reading Association. He has been recognized as a distinguished professor, writer, and outstanding teacher educator. He has taught students from kindergarten through college and serves as a consultant and speaker to schools and professional organizations.

Dr. Johns is a past president of the Illinois Reading Council, College Reading Association, and Northern Illinois Reading Council. He has received recognition for outstanding service to each of these professional organizations and is a member of the Illinois Reading Council Hall of Fame. Dr. Johns has served on numerous committees of the International Reading Association (IRA) and was a member of the Board of Directors. He has also received the Outstanding Teacher Educator in Reading Award from the International Reading Association.

Dr. Johns has been invited to consult, conduct workshops, and make presentations for teachers and professional groups throughout the United States and Canada. He has also prepared nearly 300 publications that have been useful to a diverse group of educators. His *Basic Reading Inventory*, now in its eighth edition, is widely used in undergraduate and graduate classes, as well as by practicing teachers. Dr. Johns recently coauthored the third edition of *Improving Reading: Strategies and Resources* and a new volume titled *Strategies for Content Area Learning: Vocabulary, Comprehension, and Response.*

Roberta L. (Bobbi) Berglund has had a long and distinguished career in education. Her public school experience spans more than twenty years and includes serving as a classroom teacher, reading specialist, Title I Director, and district curriculum administrator. Dr. Berglund has been a member of the reading faculty at the University of Wisconsin-Whitewater and has also taught graduate reading courses at Northern Illinois University, Rockford College, National-Louis University, and Aurora University. Currently Dr. Berglund is a consultant in the area of reading and language arts, working with school districts and regional offices of education in developing curriculum and assessments, conducting staff development, and guiding the selection of instructional materials for reading, spelling, writing, and related areas.

Dr. Berglund has received honors for outstanding service to several organizations and has been selected as a member of the Illinois Reading Council Hall of Fame. She also was honored with the Those Who Excel Award from the Illinois State Board of Education.

Dr. Berglund has served on several committees of the International Reading Association, including the program committee for the World Congress in Scotland and as chair of the Publications Committee. She has worked extensively with an international team of reading professionals to develop an on-line electronic journal and, most recently, has participated in the development of an early literacy assessment.

Dr. Berglund has conducted numerous workshops for teachers and has been invited to make presentations at state, national, and international conferences. She is the author of over fifty publications and is the coauthor of three professional books, including *Strategies for Content Area Learning: Vocabulary, Comprehension, and Response.* Current projects include conducting research on kindergarten assessment practices and working with professionals to reconceptualize literacy instruction in first grade classrooms.

1. What Is Fluency?

Reading fluency is the ability to read with accuracy, expression, comprehension, and appropriate rate. According to the National Reading Panel (2000, p. 3-1), fluency is reading text "with speed, accuracy, and proper expression." Harris and Hodges (1995) also consider comprehension to be an essential aspect of fluency.

Although fluency pertains to both oral and silent reading, fluency is often associated with oral reading, because teachers can observe accuracy by recording the number of miscues the student makes while reading and can also note the student's rate, phrasing, and expression. Generally, it is assumed that oral reading is similar, but not identical, to students' silent reading. Speed and comprehension can be evaluated in both oral and silent reading. You might find it useful to think of fluency as having four components: 1) speed, 2) accuracy, 3) appropriate expression, and 4) comprehension.

Speed refers to rate of reading, usually determined in words per minute (WPM) or words correct per minute (WCPM). In question 4, we will show you how to determine a student's reading speed.

Accuracy means that the student recognizes most words automatically with little effort or attention. It should be expected that students will make some miscues (for example, mispronouncing, omitting, or inserting words) during reading. If the student misses more than 10% of the words in a passage (one word in ten), the text or material is probably too difficult to use for instruction (Johns, 2001).

Appropriate expression means that the student uses phrasing, tone, and pitch so that oral reading sounds conversational. Prosody (prŏs´ ə-dē) is the term commonly used for these elements (Dowhower, 1991). Note the slashes in the following sentence; they provide an example of what proper expression would approximate when read aloud.

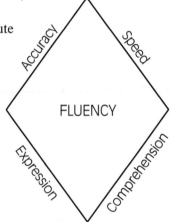

The Components of Fluency

> *The frisky dog/ ran quickly/ to the front door.*

Comprehension refers to understanding. Without comprehension, reading is merely word calling or barking at print. Comprehension is usually evaluated through retellings, answering questions, discussions, drawing/art, dramatic interpretation, or some combination of these methods. Fluency is related to reading comprehension, so helping students read quickly, accurately, and smoothly helps improve comprehension (National Reading Panel, 2000; Pinnell, Pikulski, Wixson, Campbell, Gough, & Beatty, 1995). The four components of fluency are shown in the illustration.

2. Why Is Fluency Important?

In essence, students who are fluent readers are better able to devote their attention to comprehending the text. LaBerge and Samuels (1974) presented the basic theory underlying fluency. A student has only so much attention to focus on comprehension. As more and more of that attention is devoted to recognizing words, the result is likely to be limited reading fluency and comprehension. Fluency, then, generally results in increased comprehension.

There are other reasons why fluency is important. Students who experience difficulty in reading, for the most part, lack fluency. To help students who struggle in reading, attention in the instructional program should be devoted to fluency. "It is generally acknowledged that fluency is a critical component of skilled reading" (National Reading Panel, 2000a, p. 3-1). For example, Shanahan (2000), in his framework for literacy instruction, identifies fluency as one of the major components. Heilman, Blair, and Rupley (2002) also identify fluency as a major instructional task. Fluency with text also helps to affirm and support the student's positive perception as a reader.

3. Does Fluency Apply to Silent Reading?

Yes. As discussed earlier, fluency is often thought about in relation to oral reading; nevertheless, fluency is also important in silent reading if students are to be efficient and effective readers. Silent reading also becomes more important as students move through the grades. Ultimately, most of the reading done by students and adults is silent reading. Because silent reading is used so commonly, the rate at which students comprehend is an important instructional consideration.

Carver (1989) has provided some helpful information on silent reading rates. The figures he provides are the average reading rates of students in a particular grade who can understand material at that grade level. Note that rate is considered in tandem with comprehension or understanding. Carver presents his rate figures in standard word lengths, but you can determine a student's rate (which we answer in the next question) and compare it to the figures in Table 1. Such a comparison will give you an indication of how the student's rate compares with the rates at which average students in a particular grade read with understanding.

Table 1 Silent Reading Rates for Students in Various Grades Who Understand the Material

Grade	1	2	3	4	5
WPM	<81	82–108	109–130	131–147	148–161

6	7	8	9	10	11	12
162–174	175–185	186–197	198–209	210–224	225–240	241–255

4. How Is Rate of Reading Determined?

Reading rate is often reported in words per minute (WPM). The same procedure can be used for oral and silent reading. Basically, the procedure involves having the student read a selection while you time the reading, using a stopwatch or a watch with a second hand. The following steps will permit you to determine a student's rate of reading in WPM.

1. Count or estimate the number of words in the selection. If the passage is short (175 words or less), actually count the words. If the passage is longer, you can estimate the number of words by counting the number of words on a representative line of text and counting the number of lines. Then you multiply the two numbers to get an estimate of the number of words in the passage. For example, if there are 30 lines in the passage, with 10 words on

a representative line, there would be approximately 300 words (30 × 10 = 300) in the passage.

2. Multiply by 60 (300 × 60 = 18000). This step is necessary to determine WPM.

3. This numeral becomes the dividend (18000).

4. Time the student's reading in seconds (e.g., 90 seconds).

5. This numeral becomes the divisor (90).

6. Do the necessary division. The resulting numeral is the quotient, which is words per minute (WPM).

Example
1. 300
2. 18000
3.)18000
4. 90
5. 90)18000
6. 90)18000 200 WPM
          180

If the resulting numeral is based on silent reading, use Table 1 from question 3. If the student reads orally, use either Table 2, Table 3, or Table 4 presented in the answer to the next question.

5. What Oral Reading Rates Are Appropriate for Different Grade Levels?

The answer to this straightforward question is more complex than it appears. One reason for this complexity is that there is no consensus in the literature (Bear & Barone, 1998; Rasinski & Padak, 1996). Another reason is that classrooms and schools can differ in many variables that impact so-called average oral reading rates. Perhaps the best advice is to develop local rates for different grade levels. Such advice, however, means more work for school personnel. The results of such efforts, if undertaken in a thoughtful and consistent manner, will provide meaningful and useful data. To help teachers who may not have the time or desire to establish local norms for oral reading rates, we provide three tables that may be useful.

Table 2 is based on a five-year study by Forman and Sanders (1998), who established norms for first-grade students. Their procedure, in each of the district's 14 schools, involved randomly selecting students who were judged by their teachers to be making average grade-level progress in reading. Any students recommended for special reading services, special education, or believed to be reading above grade level were excluded from the study. Over a five-year period, Forman and Sanders had first graders read stories while an examiner recorded miscues and the number of seconds it took for reading. Stories with increasing levels of difficulty were read throughout the school year. Mean accuracy (in percentage of

Table 2 Mean Oral Reading Rates for "On-Grade Level" First Graders

Months	Number of Students	Mean Accuracy	Mean Rate* (WPM)	Standard Deviation
Dec.–Jan.	1,173	95%	54	22
Feb.–March	1,192	96%	66	24
April–May	1,166	96%	79	26

*Reported in words per minute

words pronounced correctly) and reading rate in WPM (words per minute) were determined for over 1,100 students for each of the three time periods (December–January, February–March, and April–May). The results of the study are reported in Table 2. These norms may be useful to teachers who wish to have some empirical standards for the mean reading rates of average first-grade students at various points in the first-grade year.

Keep in mind that these rates of reading, based on a total of over 3,500 students, are from a single, large, suburban school district whose students generally score above average on state and national reading assessments. The standard deviations give some indication of the wide range of reading rates among first-grade students. Adding and subtracting one standard deviation (e.g., 26) to the mean rate of 79 WPM means that approximately two-thirds of the students will have rates between 53 and 95 WPM in April and May of first grade. The wide variation of reading rates suggests that these norms should be used with caution.

Hasbrouck and Tindal (1992) have provided large-scale norms for students' oral reading rates in grades two through five. These norms were developed by having students read passages at sight for one minute from their grade-level texts, regardless of the students' instructional levels. Because most classrooms have students who represent a wide range of reading levels, their procedure resulted in some students reading passages that were presumed to be easy (independent level), while other students were asked to read passages that would be too difficult (frustration level). The resulting norms, shown in Table 3, are based on over 7,000 students. The norms provide "words correct per minute" at the 75th, 50th, and 25th percentiles for students in grades two through five at three points (fall, winter, and spring) in the school year. Because the norms are reported in words correct per minute (WCPM), comparing them to the WPM as determined in this book means that there is a slightly different basis for comparison. Comparisons can still be

Table 3 Median Oral Reading Rates for Students in Grades Two through Five

Grade	Percentile	Fall WCPM*	Winter WCPM	Spring WCPM
2	75	82	106	124
	50	53	78	94
	25	23	46	65
3	75	107	123	142
	50	79	93	114
	25	65	70	87
4	75	125	133	143
	50	99	112	118
	25	72	89	92
5	75	126	143	151
	50	105	118	128
	25	77	93	100

*Reported in words correct per minute

done and subsequently used to make informal appraisals regarding the student's rate of reading. Just remember that the rates in Table 3 are more conservative than the rates determined by the WPM method. The percentiles within each grade level can be used informally to help you track and monitor student progress within a particular grade and to compare student growth in WPM to established standards.

Norms for grades six through eight are based on over 3,500 students reading passages developed for general outcome measurement (Howe & Shinn, 2001). These norms provide words correct per minute for the 90th, 75th, 50th, 25th, and 10th percentiles at three points in the school year. You may use the norms presented in Table 4 to help track and monitor student progress when compared to established standards. Keep in mind, however, that the norms for eighth grade are based on fewer than 500 students (www.edformation.com); moreover, the norms are from several school districts in Minnesota.

Table 4 Oral Reading Rates for Students in Grades Six through Eight

Grade	Percentile	Fall WCPM*	Winter WCPM	Spring WCPM
	90	171	185	201
	75	143	160	172
6	50	115	132	145
	25	91	106	117
	10	73	81	90
	90	200	207	213
	75	175	183	193
7	50	147	158	167
	25	126	134	146
	10	106	116	124
	90	208	217	221
	75	183	196	198
8	50	156	167	171
	25	126	144	145
	10	100	113	115

*Reported in words correct per minute

6. What Are Some Ways to Assess Fluency?

We suggest a combination of quantitative (numbers) and qualitative (behaviors) criteria. There are often numbers related to reading rate expressed in words per minute (WPM). Tables 1, 2, 3, and 4 contain numbers that can be used in a quantitative manner. You can also keep track of how accurately a student reads by counting the number of miscues (e.g., mispronunciations, repetitions, insertions, substitutions, and omissions) made during the reading of a passage. The method of Structured Repeated Readings, described in Part 2 of this book, offers one way to help judge a student's progress, as the same passage is reread over a period of days.

Additional behaviors that can be noted are listed below.

- voice quality
- expression and emphasis
- phrasing and pauses
- appropriate use of punctuation

Some teachers develop an informal fluency rubric that can be used to judge qualitative aspects of fluency. We have provided one such rubric (5-Point Fluency Scale) on page 9 that you may wish to use.

The Classroom Fluency Snapshot (CFS), developed by Blachowicz, Sullivan, and Cieply (2001), offers another way to assess fluency. This assessment shows clearly how a student's reading rate compares with others in the classroom. The CFS can be used in the fall of the school year to help establish baseline data for the class. Subsequent snapshots can be used throughout the year to measure and monitor student progress. The chart in the sidebar to the right shows an example from a second-grade classroom. Below is an adapted step-by-step procedure for using the CFS with a class of students.

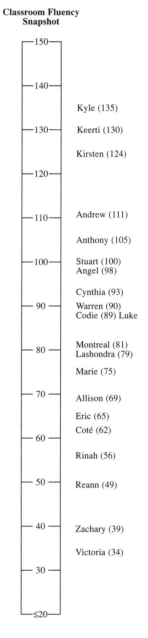

Classroom Fluency Snapshot

1. Select a passage that is representative of the material you will use for instruction. All students will read the same passage, so make sufficient copies for the class. The majority of students should be able to read the passage with at least 85% to 90% initial accuracy. Choose a passage that will take students one or two minutes to read. Although the passage will be difficult for some of your poorer readers, you will be able to establish baseline data for the entire class. You will need:
   - a copy of the passage for the student to read.
   - a copy of the passage on which you will mark miscues (any deviation from what's written) such as omissions, insertions, mispronunciations, ignoring or adding punctuation, and words pronounced after waiting four seconds. You may mark the actual miscues where they occur in the text, if you are familiar with coding miscues or use a running record procedure. If you are not experienced with coding miscues, merely make a check mark over the miscue. A method for coding miscues can be found in Johns (2001).
   - a stopwatch or a watch with a second hand to time the student's reading.
   - a tape recorder if you wish to do the analysis later or recheck your coding of miscues and the number of seconds taken for reading.

2. Invite individual students to read the passage to you. You could offer an introductory statement like: "Please read this passage about _____ at a speed that's just right for you. Read as accurately as you can. When you have finished reading, I'll ask you a few questions (or I'll ask you to retell what you have read)." At the end of one minute, make a mark after the last word read by the student. Invite a short retelling or ask some questions based on the selection.

3. Count the number of words read in one minute and then subtract the number of miscues (e.g., mispronunciations, insertions, and ignoring punctuation). An easy way to determine word counts is to place a numeral at the end of each line to indicate the cumulative number of words. Use this information to quickly determine the number of words the student read and then subtract the number of miscues to determine words correct per minute. A partial sample is shown in the box on page 10.

5-Point Fluency Scale for Oral Reading

Student _____ Grade _____ Teacher _____

	1	2	3	4	5
	Word-by-word	Some word-by-word, some 2–3 word phrases	Phrases; some word-by-word	Mostly in phrases	Phrasing consistently used
	Long pauses between words; struggles with words	Some hesitations; sounds out words; disrupts flow	Some smooth, some choppy	Generally smooth; may exhibit difficulty with some words	Generally smooth; good use of self-corrections
	Reads in monotone	Reads mostly in monotone	Combines use of expression with monotone	Appropriate expression used throughout much of the piece	Appropriate expression; intonation maintained throughout
	Little evidence of use of punctuation	Shows some use of punctuation	Shows some use of punctuation, but still ignores some	Use of punctuation is generally good	Uses punctuation consistently
	Rate is generally slow and laborious	Slow rate	Rate varies	Rate is generally conversational	Rate is conversational and consistent throughout

Date	Level	Selection	Comments

From Jerry L. Johns and Roberta L. Berglund, *Fluency: Questions, Answers, and Evidence-Based Strategies*. Copyright © 2002 Kendall/Hunt Publishing Company (1-800-247-3458, ext. 5). May be reproduced for noncommercial educational purposes.

```
                              At the Farm
                          about          wanted
            Sue was visiting her grandparents' farm for a week. She decided to have a picnic      15
        in the woods. She packed a lunch with a peanut-butter and jelly sandwich, an apple,       31

            The
        When she remembered/Jane. She ran back to the house and got Jane, her favorite doll.     108
                  'end of
                   one minute

        Name _____ Date _____

        Total Words Read   ___95___  Additional Notes/Comments:   good phrasing
        Number of Miscues __3___
        Words per Minute  ___92___
```

4. Compile the results for all the students on a sample chart like that shown on page 8 to see the range of rates in your class and to help determine which students might profit from instruction to increase fluency. Repeating the process several times during the school year (see page 11) with different passages should enable you to assess individual and class progress. The blank charts on pages 12–13 are provided for your use. One chart is for the primary grades; the other chart is for the upper grades. They can be used to chart classroom data in a manner similar to that on the following page.

7. What's Wrong with Round Robin Oral Reading?

Round robin oral reading is "the outmoded practice of calling on students to read orally one after the other" (Harris & Hodges, 1995, p. 222). It often refers to oral reading done at sight in the context of whole class or small group instruction and looks something like this: "Class, turn to page 53 in your books. José, you begin reading. I want the rest of the class to follow along." As José reads, some students are reading ahead, some are actually following along, and others are looking out the window or daydreaming. You may even recall some of your own experiences with round robin oral reading. Rarely are positive comments shared about the practice (Johns & Galen, 1977).

So what's wrong with this practice? Here's our list of common objections to the practice of round robin oral reading:

- It focuses mostly on oral reading performance, rather than understanding.
- It rarely engages students (except the student who is reading).
- It has little connection to reading in real life.
- It reduces the time that could be better spent on quality instructional practices.
- It teaches students very little.
- It is embarrassing to poorer readers.

> Round robin oral reading rarely fulfills the purposes of oral reading.

Reading Rates in WPM for Grade Two Classroom

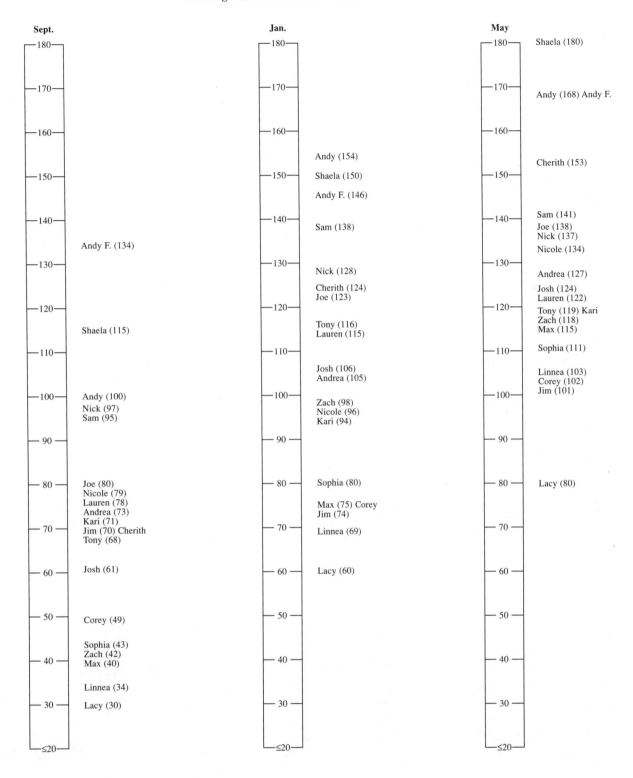

Sept.

- 180
- 170
- 160
- 150
- 140
- 130 — Andy F. (134)
- 120 — Shaela (115)
- 110
- 100 — Andy (100) / Nick (97) / Sam (95)
- 90
- 80 — Joe (80) / Nicole (79) / Lauren (78) / Andrea (73) / Kari (71)
- 70 — Jim (70) Cherith / Tony (68)
- 60 — Josh (61)
- 50 — Corey (49)
- 40 — Sophia (43) / Zach (42) / Max (40)
- — Linnea (34)
- 30 — Lacy (30)
- ≤20

Jan.

- 180
- 170
- 160
- 150 — Andy (154) / Shaela (150) / Andy F. (146)
- 140 — Sam (138)
- 130 — Nick (128) / Cherith (124) / Joe (123)
- 120 — Tony (116) / Lauren (115)
- 110 — Josh (106) / Andrea (105)
- 100 — Zach (98) / Nicole (96) / Kari (94)
- 90
- 80 — Sophia (80)
- — Max (75) Corey / Jim (74)
- 70 — Linnea (69)
- 60 — Lacy (60)
- 50
- 40
- 30
- ≤20

May

- 180 — Shaela (180)
- 170 — Andy (168) Andy F.
- 160
- 150 — Cherith (153)
- 140 — Sam (141) / Joe (138) / Nick (137) / Nicole (134)
- 130 — Andrea (127)
- 120 — Josh (124) / Lauren (122) / Tony (119) Kari / Zach (118) / Max (115)
- 110 — Sophia (111)
- — Linnea (103) / Corey (102) / Jim (101)
- 100
- 90
- 80 — Lacy (80)
- 70
- 60
- 50
- 40
- 30
- ≤20

Class Fluency Record—Primary Grades

Teacher_____ Grade _____

Date_____   Date_____   Date_____

Passage_____   Passage_____   Passage_____

180	180	180
170	170	170
160	160	160
150	150	150
140	140	140
130	130	130
120	120	120
110	110	110
100	100	100
90	90	90
80	80	80
70	70	70
60	60	60
50	50	50
40	40	40
30	30	30
≤20	≤20	≤20

Class Fluency Record—Upper Grades

Teacher _____ Grade _____

Date _____   Date _____   Date _____

Passage _____   Passage _____   Passage _____

220	220	220
210	210	210
200	200	200
190	190	190
180	180	180
170	170	170
160	160	160
150	150	150
140	140	140
130	130	130
120	120	120
110	110	110
100	100	100
90	90	90
80	80	80
70	70	70
60	60	60
≤50	≤50	≤50

According to Hyatt (1943), who traced the history and development of oral reading over a sixty-year period, oral reading is worthwhile only when it 1) informs or entertains an audience; 2) enables students to participate in a group activity (such as choral reading); or 3) increases one's personal pleasure by reading aloud beautiful passages of literature. Unfortunately, round robin oral reading rarely, if ever, fulfills any of these three purposes.

When it comes to fluency, there is no doubt that **meaningful oral reading is important**. A study by Eldredge, Reutzel, and Hollingsworth (1996) found that round robin oral reading was inferior to the shared book experience in reducing students' miscues, improving reading fluency, increasing vocabulary acquisition, and improving reading comprehension. In Part 2 of this book, we will offer a number of oral reading practices that promote fluency without the negatives generally associated with round robin oral reading.

8. What Part of the Reading Program Should Be Devoted to Fluency Instruction?

In the position statement of the International Reading Association (2000, p. 3), "the ability to read fluently" is among the skills students need to become readers. Shanahan (2000a) suggests that up to 25% of the instructional time for reading should be focused on fluency instruction. That percentage may be high, but it is clear that fluency is one aspect of the reading program that is often neglected (Allington, 1983a; Teale & Shanahan, 2001). The amount of time devoted to fluency instruction may depend on the grade level and the student's facility with word identification.

> The ability to read fluently is among the skills students need to become readers.

In the primary literacy standards, fluency is a standard in kindergarten, first grade, and second grade (New Standards Primary Literacy Committee, 1999). Descriptions of fluency examples for each of these three grades follows.

Kindergarten—Shiori reads a 78-word book with adequate intonation. She pauses appropriately for periods at the end of each sentence and points to each word as she reads. "Although an adult reader might put more punctuation and drama into the reading to make it more interesting, Shiori's reading is considered fluent for the end of kindergarten" (New Standards Primary Literacy Committee, 1999, p. 59).

First Grade—Christopher reads a 279-word story fluently. "He could pause more appropriately at commas when they appear just before a quotation mark. Although he usually drops his voice to note the ends of sentences, the drop could be more emphatic" (New Standards Primary Literacy Committee, 1999, p. 100). Christopher's reading is basically fluent for the end of first grade because he sounds like he knows what he is reading.

Second Grade—Griffin reads a 631-word story "fluently as far as clear and correct pronunciation of words is concerned. His verbal emphasis on words and phrases signals the meaning of the text. However, his intonation and phrasing could be improved. He does not pause long enough within sections of dialogue to signal the end of the speaker's words. Sometimes he runs from one sentence right into another" (New Standards Literacy Committee, 1999, p. 147). Griffin's reading is considered fluent for the end of second grade.

As students move beyond second grade, they should continue to exhibit attention to punctuation, good intonation, appropriate phrasing, good voice quality, and dialogue. Because more and more of the students' reading will be done silently, these particular behaviors can be observed in contexts when oral reading is appropriate. Many of those contexts are presented in Part 2.

9. What Insights from Fluency Can Be Drawn from Research and Expert Opinion?

An analysis of the National Assessment of Educational Progress data revealed that approximately 44% of students were unable to read grade-level material with adequate fluency (Pinnell, Pikulski, Wixson, Campbell, Gough, & Beatty, 1995). In recent years, there has been increased emphasis on research-based and evidenced-based practices related to reading. Kuhn and Stahl (2000) reviewed over forty studies related to fluency and concluded that "both assisted and unassisted methods of fluency instruction have been generally effective in facilitating rate and accuracy" (p. 25). Some of the studies also found improvements in students' comprehension.

> Repeated oral reading with feedback and guidance leads to improvements in reading.

After reviewing many studies, the contributors to the Report of the National Reading Panel (2000) noted that fluency can be improved for good readers as well as readers who struggle. "Classroom practices that encourage repeated oral reading with feedback and guidance lead to meaningful improvements in reading expertise for students" (National Reading Panel, 2000, p. 3-3). One way to judge the impact of guided oral reading procedures is to look at the effect size—the extent to which performance of the treatment group is greater than the performance of the control group. Effect sizes can be small (.20), moderate (.50), or large (.80). Table 5 shows the effect sizes for reading accuracy, fluency, and comprehension. "These data provide strong support for the supposition that instruction in guided oral reading is effective in improving reading" (National Reading Panel, 2000, p. 3-3).

Table 5 Effect Sizes of Repeated Oral Reading with Feedback on Three Reading Outcomes

Reading Outcome	Effect Size
Reading Accuracy	.55
Reading Fluency	.44
Reading Comprehension	.35

Klenk and Kibby (2000) also reviewed fluency research. They found that repeated reading was a common method of developing fluency, especially for students in the primary grades. They also noted that teacher modeling of the text students were about to read was another practice used to promote fluency. There are also many research studies (see Pearson & Fielding, 1991, for a review) that have shown relationships between the amount of reading students engage in and reading achievement. That finding suggests that recreational reading and other independent reading (like sustained silent reading) in and out of school are important considerations in any efforts to increase fluency. Some specific procedures were also mentioned in the reviews of research (repeated reading, neurological impress, radio reading, and paired reading), so we have included them in Part 2 of the book.

10. What Factors Can Impact Fluency?

The most fundamental and important basis for fluency is accuracy in word recognition. The significance of this area was pointed out by Anderson, Hiebert, Scott, and Wilkinson (1985), who noted that "one of the cornerstones of skilled reading is fast, accurate word identification." When the student recognizes most of the words quickly and easily, they are called sight words. The larger a student's sight vocabulary, the greater the likelihood that reading will be fluent. While automatic word recognition is necessary, it is not a sufficient indicator of fluent reading.

Other factors can also impact fluency:

- Reading widely and often provides practice to solidify skills and helps promote confidence in reading.
- Opportunities to participate in meaningful activities for oral reading provide helpful models and practice.
- Listening to teachers read aloud on a daily basis provides an excellent model, enlarges students' vocabularies (Elley, 1988; Layne, 1996), and helps promote the value of reading.

There are also many direct and indirect actions you can take to teach and promote fluency. We present many of these actions, lessons, and tips in Part 2.

> The most important basis for fluency is accuracy in word recognition.

11. When Should Fluency Instruction Begin?

According to Kuhn and Stahl's review of research involving practices for developmental and remedial readers (2000), students need to have some basic reading ability before focusing on fluency. Generally, this ability involves knowledge of sight vocabulary and an understanding of how print works. Students typically achieve this ability at the late pre-primer level. Older students who read at a late second-grade level or lower can also profit from fluency instruction. In addition, Worthy and Broaddus (2001/2002) note that fluency practice can also be used with older students to contribute to their comprehension and enjoyment of a wide range of textual materials.

> Students need to have some basic reading ability before focusing on fluency.

12. What Are the Basic Principles of Fluency Instruction?

Our review of the research, extensive reading, and professional experience led to the formulation of the following set of foundational principles related to fluency instruction.

1.   Fluency is one of three core elements of skilled reading; the other two are identifying words and constructing meaning. For students, fluency is the

bridge or link between the ability to identify words quickly and the ability to understand text. It is an "important but often overlooked aspect of reading" (Strickland, Ganske, & Monroe, 2002, p. 120). If students read fluently, they can focus most of their attention on the meaningful and enjoyable aspects of reading (Burns, Griffin, & Snow, 1999). The illustration below shows the role fluency plays in skilled reading.

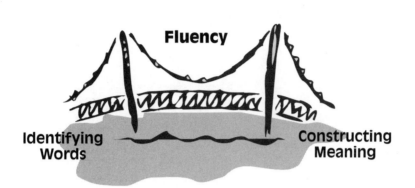

Fluency

Identifying Words   **Constructing Meaning**

Fluency is the bridge between the ability to identify words and the ability to understand text.

2. Fluency is linked to comprehension. The impact of oral reading practice, feedback, and guidance on comprehension "is not inconsiderable, and in several comparisons it was actually quite high" (National Reading Panel, 2000, p. 3-18). Although there is reason to believe that oral reading practice and feedback have an impact on comprehension, we want to stress the importance of assessing comprehension or inviting retellings. Students need to understand that the goal of reading is the construction of meaning—not merely pronouncing words quickly and accurately. We want students to be meaning seekers who are able to read words quickly and easily.

Students need to understand that the goal of reading is meaning.

3. Fluency develops from practice (National Reading Panel, 2000). There is no substitute for an abundance of reading from a wide variety of printed materials. In Part 2 of the book, we offer a range of activities to help students practice reading. Some of the methods involve individual reading, partner reading, sharing in small groups, and whole class activities. A key feature of the practice is multiple readings. Such readings help build fluency and confidence.

4. Fluency is dependent on a variety of factors. The difficulty, complexity, and interest level of the materials used for instruction and practice impact fluency. Ideally, materials should be appropriate in difficulty and of interest to students. Helpful sources of leveled books for use in kindergarten through sixth grade have been developed by Fountas and Pinnell (2000, 2001).

A key feature of fluency practice is multiple readings of text.

5. Fluency can be improved by teaching. Modeling, demonstrating, and thinking out loud are some of the explicit actions teachers can take to help students become fluent readers. Teachers can model fluent reading and take time to discuss what makes reading fluent. Teaching phrasing and providing guided practice will also help remove some of the mystery of fluency. In short, teachers have to be ready to be explicit with their instruction when it is necessary. Systematic teaching will not leave the skill of fluency to chance. In the words of Teale and Shanahan (2001, p. 8), "there are few positive changes as straightforward and potentially productive as an appropriate focus on fluency. It is time for us to stop ignoring the essential and to teach fluency as a regular part of our reading programs."

Evidence-Based Strategies, Activities, and Resources

Overview   20
Classroom Instruction   22
Assisted Reading   48
Independent Practice   65

OVERVIEW

This part of the book contains instructional principles, strategies, activities, and resources to help students become fluent readers. We begin with four foundational principles to guide your teaching.

1. Match Students' Reading Abilities to Appropriate Materials for Instruction

Instruction is likely to be more effective when there is an appropriate match between a student's reading level and the material used for instruction or practice. This match is typically referred to as the student's instructional level (Johns, 2001). At the instructional level, the student generally misses no more than one word in twenty (95% accuracy) and satisfactorily understands what was read. The implication of this principle is that teachers will use a variety of materials at different levels in the instructional program, so students are able to read with success. According to Burns (2001), a critical foundation of guided reading is that students read materials at their respective instructional levels. But as Opitz and Ford (2001) point out, matching texts with students "is anything but simple. The interaction among texts, readers, and reading contexts is highly complex and involves a number of variable factors." It is clear, however, that students should spend the majority of time with reading materials at their instructional (just right) level.

2. Model Oral Reading

Daily oral reading to students should be an integral part of the instructional program. Many professionals agree that reading orally to students:

- stimulates language development.
- helps students move naturally into reading.
- shows that reading is pleasurable.
- demonstrates that print is meaningful.
- fosters an interest in printed materials.
- stimulates students to react to what is read.
- helps develop favorable attitudes toward reading.
- encourages students to listen actively.
- serves as a model.
- builds rapport.
- shares the joy of reading.
- helps enlarge vocabulary.

With respect to fluency, students will hear you share how oral reading should sound. Phrasing, emphasis, and tone are some of the aspects of fluency that can be modeled through regular periods of reading aloud.

3. Provide Guided Oral Reading Opportunities

There are a number of guided oral reading procedures (e.g., radio reading, paired reading) in which teachers are typically involved, especially as they are initially introduced and modeled. The impact of such teaching, modeling, and feedback results in student learning. The National Reading Panel (2000) concluded that such procedures had a consistent and positive impact on word recognition, fluency, and comprehension for a wide range of readers over a wide range of levels (i.e., first grade through college). Later in Part 2, we provide a number of ways you can provide repeated oral reading opportunities for students to improve fluency and overall reading achievement.

4. Offer Daily Opportunities for Students to Read Easy Materials Independently

The amount of time students spend in silent reading in the average classroom is small. "An estimate of silent reading in the typical primary school class is 7 or 8 minutes per day, or less than 10% of the total time devoted to reading. By the middle grades, silent reading time may average 15 minutes per school day" (Anderson, Hiebert, Scott, & Wilkinson, 1985, p. 76).

The National Reading Panel (2000) considered "all formal efforts to increase the amounts of independent or recreational reading" by students. Such reading should typically involve materials that are easy for the student. Materials at the student's easy or independent level are read with a high degree of accuracy (98% or more) and excellent comprehension (Johns, 2001).

One popular and widely used effort to promote independent reading is sustained silent reading (Hunt, 1970) described on page 66. Providing a daily period for students to read easy materials independently:

- helps establish the habit of reading.
- provides an opportunity for practice.
- promotes a love of reading.
- communicates the importance of reading.
- familiarizes students with many types of reading materials.
- encourages the selection of appropriate reading materials.
- helps get reluctant readers into books.
- allows freedom for students to self-select reading materials.
- has a settling effect in the classroom.
- fosters engagement with printed materials.

While research reviewed by the National Reading Panel (2000) did not clearly and convincingly establish the impact of independent reading on overall reading achievement, the Panel concluded that independent reading might be beneficial. "There is an extensive amount of correlational data [hundreds of studies] linking amount of reading and reading achievement" (National Reading Panel, 2000). In our professional judgment, therefore, voluntary reading is worthwhile, even if much of the evidence is correlational. We would not want to see less voluntary reading in classrooms.

Classroom Instruction

Basic Sight Words   23

Language Experience   27

Shared Book Experience   29

Echo Reading   31

Choral Reading   32

Antiphonal Reading   33

Readers Theater   35

Radio Reading   37

Oral Recitation Lesson   40

Fluency Development Lesson   42

Say It Like the Character   43

Super Signals   45

Phrase Boundaries   47

Basic Sight Words

DESCRIPTION

There are about 200 basic sight words that occur over and over in the English language (Johns, 1976). These words can comprise over 60% of the words used in beginning reading materials and over 50% of the words used in materials in the upper grades and beyond (including materials read by adults). This explains why the words are commonly referred to as *basic, high-frequency*, or *function* words. Students need to know these words automatically if they are to become fluent readers. Such words are a necessary, but not sufficient, condition for efficient reading. They are often difficult for students to learn because many of the words look similar, are abstract, and are not considered "regular" in pronunciation. Two basic word lists are provided for your use. The Revised Dolch List (1976) and High-Frequency Nouns (Johns, 1975) can be found on page 25 and page 26 respectively. They provide words for teaching and practice. Below are some tips for teaching and practicing basic sight words. Several additional strategies are offered by Johns, Lenski, and Elish-Piper (2002).

IDEAS FOR INSTRUCTION AND PRACTICE

1. *Create Instructional Materials.* Use words from the Revised Dolch List and the High-Frequency Nouns to create phrases, sentences, and short stories that students can read and reread to learn the words and gain confidence. You might want to invite older students to use the lists to prepare materials that can be used by their peers or younger students in a different grade. The phrases and sentences can be written on cards. The stories can be bound into simple little books and illustrated by the student who authored the book or the student who reads the book. Provide repeated opportunities for students to read the materials individually, with partners, and at home. Stress the need to read accurately with expression. Model as needed. Examples are shown below.

Phrases

by the road

over by the school

Sentences

What time of the year is it?

Her work was done very well.

That thing has two heads!

Short Story (A little book with a line on each page)

My Father

I have a father.
He is a good man.
He works in a big city.
He gives me money.
Next year, he will get a new blue car.
It is time for me to go home from school.
My father will be at home.
He is going to get me a little dog.
The dog will be a good friend.
My father and I will play with him.
What should I call my dog?

2. *Use Pattern Books.* Select a particular pattern book that contains the word or words you want to help students to learn or practice. There are many pattern books, and a large listing of such books can be found in Johns and Lenski (2001). Read the book aloud to students and, if possible, use a big book version so students can follow along. Reread the book, inviting students to read along, as they are able. You may wish to point to each word as it is read. Provide opportunities for students to take turns reading the book to each other. Later, you could prepare sentence strips with words from the pattern book and invite students to read the text from the sentence strips. The sentence strips could be cut up, and students could rearrange the words in order and read the sentence. Stress the need for meaningful phrasing and attention to punctuation. Older students could be invited to share some of the pattern books with younger students, thus helping to develop reader confidence.

3. *Teach Words Explicitly.* Students may persistently misread some of the basic sight words. Note the troublesome words and develop lessons to teach the words. Write the word on the chalkboard; students can write the word on a card. Chant the word. Then spell the word and say it as a class two or three times (e.g., w-e-n-t, went, w-e-n-t, went, w-e-n-t, went). Write several sentences on the chalkboard with a blank space for the word being learned. Invite students to read the sentence silently and then ask a volunteer to print the missing words in the sentence. Have the sentence read aloud, using good phrasing and expression. You should also model for students as needed. A few examples are shared below.

Joann and Cheyenne _____ to the soccer game.

I _____ to see my friend, Javon.

I hit the ball and it _____ about ten feet!

Do you know where she _____ ?

Students can also be invited to find the troublesome words in materials they read. Because basic sight words appear frequently, help students understand that knowing such words will enable them to read more quickly and easily.

Revised Dolch List

a	could	he	might	same	told
about	cut	heard	more	saw	too
across	did	help	most	say	took
after	didn't	her	much	see	toward
again	do	here	must	she	try
all	does	high	my	short	turn
always	done	him	near	should	two
am	don't	his	need	show	under
an	down	hold	never	six	up
and	draw	hot	next	small	upon
another	eat	how	new	so	us
any	enough	I	no	some	use
are	even	I'm	not	soon	very
around	every	if	now	start	walk
as	far	in	of	still	want
ask	fast	into	off	stop	warm
at	find	is	oh	take	was
away	first	it	old	tell	we
be	five	its	on	ten	well
because	for	just	once	than	went
been	found	keep	one	that	were
before	four	kind	only	the	what
began	from	know	open	their	when
best	full	last	or	them	where
better	gave	leave	other	then	which
big	get	left	our	there	while
black	give	let	out	these	white
blue	go	light	over	they	who
both	going	like	own	think	why
bring	gone	little	play	this	will
but	good	long	put	those	with
by	got	look	ran	thought	work
call	green	made	read	three	would
came	grow	make	red	through	yes
can	had	many	right	to	yet
close	hard	may	round	today	you
cold	has	me	run	together	your
come	have	mean	said		

The rationale and research for this list are described in Johns, J.L. (1976). Updating the Dolch basic sight vocabulary. *Reading Horizons, 16,* 104–111.

From Jerry L. Johns and Roberta L. Berglund, *Fluency: Questions, Answers, and Evidence-Based Strategies.* Copyright © 2002 by Kendall/Hunt Publishing Company (1-800-247-3458, ext. 5). May be reproduced for noncommercial educational purposes.

High-Frequency Nouns

air	girl	nothing
back	group	people
book	hand	place
boy	head	road
car	home	room
children	house	school
city	man	side
day	men	table
dog	money	thing
door	morning	time
eye	mother	top
face	Mr.	town
father	Mrs.	tree
feet	name	water
friend	night	way
		year

The development of this list is described in Johns, J.L. (1975). Dolch list of common nouns—A comparison. *The Reading Teacher, 28,* 338–340.

From Jerry L. Johns and Roberta L. Berglund, *Fluency: Questions, Answers, and Evidence-Based Strategies.* Copyright © 2002 by Kendall/Hunt Publishing Company (1-800-247-3458, ext. 5). May be reproduced for noncommercial educational purposes.

Language Experience

DESCRIPTION

The Language Experience approach involves writing down what students say, then reading and rereading it with them to develop knowledge of letter-sound associations, sight words, prosody, and language (Mallon & Berglund, 1984; Stauffer, 1980; Strickland, Ganske, & Monroe, 2002). Stories created in this manner are usually placed in a prominent location in the classroom or bound into class books to be used as text material for independent reading. Students can generally read language experience stories successfully because they have participated in their development. Because the text reflects the language, culture, and experiences of the students, lessons using these materials are especially appropriate for English language learners (Herrell, 2000).

PROCEDURE

1. Gather students near an easel with chart paper or a chalkboard. Provide an experience or discuss something that is of current interest to students, such as a field trip, holiday, recent event, classroom pet, or picture.

2. As students describe the experience or topic, encourage them to use complete sentences. Repeat what is said and write it down, saying each word as you write it. Include the speaker's name as in the following example.

   Mark said, "The guinea pig was sleeping this morning."

3. After writing each sentence, read it aloud smoothly and expressively. Ask the speaker, "Is this what you meant to say? Did I write it the way you said it?" Make changes as needed. Invite students to read the sentence with you.

4. Invite students to dictate additional sentences. Reread them to and with students. Additional comments about the guinea pig might be as follows.

   Emily said, "I hope it is OK."

   Erica added, "I had a guinea pig once and it slept during the day, too."

   Jerry said, "I don't think we should worry. He is probably OK."

   Tyrone said, "Let's look at him again tomorrow and see if he is asleep again."

   "If he is, I think we will feel better," offered Shaunice.

5. When the story appears to be finished, read it to students, modeling good oral reading. Ask students to read along with you. Sweep your hand under the words as they are read.

6. Ask, "Is there anything else we should add? Have we written the story just the way we want it? Do you think someone who reads the story will understand our message?" This is an important time to emphasize that reading can be talk written down, and that the purpose of speaking and writing is to communicate a message.

7. On successive days, read the story chorally (see page 32) with students. Ask individual students to choose a sentence or sentences to read aloud. If a student has difficulty with a word, provide assistance. Celebrate when students read with appropriate speed, accuracy, and expression.

8. Post the story in a prominent place in the classroom or place it in a class book so that students can read and reread it independently. Invite students to add illustrations to enhance meaning and add interest for the reader.

Shared Book Experience

DESCRIPTION

Sometimes viewed as a school version of the bedtime story, Shared Book Experience involves a teacher and a group of students sharing reading by listening to and rereading stories, rhymes, songs, and poems in an enjoyable manner (Berglund, 1988; Butler & Turbill, 1985; Holdaway, 1979). Shared Book Experience invites students into the reading process through the repeated sharing of materials that soon become favorites. Many insights about literacy can be taught from Shared Book Experiences. In order to increase visual intimacy with print, materials used for Shared Book Experiences are often enlarged books (big books) or text shared on the overhead projector. Books and stories with repetitive language patterns or predictable story structures are especially useful for this experience.

PROCEDURE

1. *Reread old favorites.* Begin with familiar rhymes, songs, poems, or chants that students know. These can be chosen either by you or by your students. Because these favorites are familiar to students, they can actively participate in the reading, particularly when there is repetitive text. For instance, for very young children, the chant, "Brown Bear, Brown Bear, What do you see?" is easily learned and repeated as the teacher reads and rereads this book (Martin, 1987). Point to the text as you read, so that students can see the print, learn print conventions (left-right, top-bottom, front-back, punctuation, spaces, title), and note the connection between written and spoken language.

2. *Introduce a new story.* At least once a week, introduce a new story. Show the cover of the text and invite students to predict what the story may be about. Share the title, author, and illustrator with students and note if other books by the same author or illustrator were shared in previous readings.

3. *Read the story aloud.* Read the story all the way through, modeling good rate and expression. You may wish to stop at exciting points and allow students to check predictions and make new ones. The purpose of this segment of the lesson is to allow students to enjoy the story.

4. *Discuss the story.* Return to the predictions made as a class and invite students to confirm or revise them. Discuss the illustrations, characters, and favorite or exciting parts of the story, to help students understand the meaning of the text. This is also a good time for students to be invited to make connections between the new story and any previous texts (text-to-text) or connections between the story and their own experiences (text-to-self) (Keene & Zimmermann, 1997).

5. *Reread the story aloud.* Invite students to join in the reading. Students may read a repetitive segment with you and add appropriate sound effects or hand gestures to enhance meaning.

6. *Make the text available for independent reading.* Put the enlarged text and/or smaller versions of the text in a reading corner or literacy center and encourage students to read it independently or with a friend.

7. *Use the text again for familiar rereadings and for teaching reading strategies.* During another Shared Book Experience, draw from the story previously read and discussed; after reading it, use the text to teach and practice the following:

   - reading with expression and fluency
   - sight vocabulary
   - sound/symbol relationships
   - word families
   - effective reading strategies

8. *Encourage students to use the meaning of the story, how the language sounds, and letter-sound relationships to predict and self-correct their reading.* Use questions such as, "Does it make sense? Does it sound right? Does it look right?" to help students develop good fix-up strategies to use when the reading process breaks down.

Fluency practice might include inviting students to Echo Read the text with you (see page 31), discussing the use of typographic signals (Super Signals on page 45), practicing Phrase Boundaries (see page 47), or using Say It Like the Character (see page 43). Following the rereading of the text, it could be used again during Sustained Silent Reading (SSR) (see page 66) or Read and Relax (see page 69). For additional ideas for using big books and Shared Book Experience, see Strickland (1993).

Echo Reading

DESCRIPTION

Echo Reading involves modeling fluent reading for students and then encouraging them to reread, or echo, the same text, with support as needed. In Echo Reading, the student immediately echoes or imitates the performance of a more skilled reader. Doing so helps the student gain confidence in reading aloud, become proficient with material that might be too difficult for the student to read independently, and practice good phrasing and expression (Allington, 2001; Gillet & Temple, 2000).

PROCEDURE

1. For students' initial experiences with echo reading, select fairly easy reading material. Stories with patterns or repeated phrases are excellent for beginning the activity. Students' language experience stories (see page 27) are also good sources for echo reading materials.
2. Read a phrase or sentence of the selection aloud. Call attention to any textual signals that help you determine the rate and expression you used. For the sentence, "'You're back!' Mama cried as her son walked through the door," you might say that the exclamation mark helped you know that you should read the sentence in an excited voice.
3. Reread the phrase or sentence and have students echo the same text immediately after you finish.
4. If students echo your reading effectively, mirroring your rate, accuracy, and expression, continue by modeling the next phrase or sentence. Then have students again echo your reading.
5. If students do not echo your reading effectively on the first try, model the phrase or sentence again and have students echo your reading again.
6. As students become proficient with easy materials, gradually move into more difficult materials.

Choral Reading

DESCRIPTION

Choral Reading involves students reading a text in unison (Gillet & Temple, 2000). It helps build confidence and extend enjoyment of the reading process (Opitz & Rasinski, 1998). Repeated practice of choral reading materials helps to develop reading competence, nurtures collaboration among students, and helps students feel successful as readers.

PROCEDURE

1. Select a text for use in the Choral Reading experience. Poetry or books with predictable story patterns, repeated phrases, or refrains work especially well. See the box below for suggested resources.
2. Provide copies of the text to each student in the group, make a transparency of the text and show it on the overhead projector or write the text on chart paper, so that all can view it.
3. Read the text aloud to students, modeling fluent reading. Tell students why you chose to read it as you did. For example, were there punctuation marks that gave you clues? Perhaps there was bold print or underlining which gave you a clue about emphasis.
4. After your modeling, invite students to follow along and read with you. Practice reading together chorally several times.
5. You may wish to vary the Choral Reading experience by having students join in chorally for repeated refrains in the text. For instance, in the poem "The Jumblies" by Edward Lear in *Sing a Song of Popcorn* by deRegniers, the refrain is one that students enjoy reading chorally, although the rest of the poem may be too difficult for them to read with fluency:

> Far and few, far and few,
> Are the lands where the Jumblies live;
> Their heads are green, and their hands are blue,
> And they went to sea in a Sieve.

6. A further adaptation of Choral Reading is Antiphonal Reading (see page 33) where students are divided into groups, with each group reading its assigned part.

Suggested Resources

Barton, B., & Booth, D. (1995). *Mother Goose goes to school*. Portland, ME: Stenhouse.

deRegniers, B. (1988). *Sing a song of popcorn: Every child's book of poems*. New York: Scholastic.

Prelutsky, J. (1984). *The new kid on the block*. New York: Greenwillow.

Prelutsky, J. (2000). *The random house book of poetry for children*. New York: Random House.

Silverstein, S. (1974). *Where the sidewalk ends*. New York: HarperCollins.

Antiphonal Reading

DESCRIPTION

Antiphonal Reading is an adaptation of choral reading. In Antiphonal Reading, students are usually divided into groups (Miccinati, 1985; Worthy & Broaddus, 2001/2002). Each group reads an assigned part—sometimes alternately, sometimes in unison. The manner of reading is cued by the placement of the text on the page. Usually Antiphonal Reading is done with poetry obtained from published sources or from materials students have created. Miccinati (1985) suggests that rhymes, limericks, sea chanties, and Indian chants are especially suited to this activity.

PROCEDURE

1. Select the text to be read and make it visually accessible by providing copies for each student or showing it on the overhead projector. Some resources are contained in the box on the following page.
2. Explain to students the unique way this material is written, for instance, in two columns, indicating how it should be read.
3. Model for students how Antiphonal Reading in two parts is done by inviting an able student who is a risk-taker to be your partner. You begin by reading the first segment of print on the left side of the page. Your partner then reads the first segment of his or her part on the right side of the page. If both sides of the page contain the same print on the same line, read that part in unison with your partner. Proceed through the entire selection, modeling good reading and the turn-taking that is involved in Antiphonal Reading. Point to the text as each of you read your respective parts so that the listeners understand the cues.
4. Now divide the students into two groups, with each group assigned either the left side or right side of the text.
5. Invite the groups to try reading the poem in the manner in which you and your partner have modeled it. Repeat the process several times, until students become proficient at reading their respective parts with fluency.
6. As a follow-up activity, you may wish to invite students to write poetry which follows the form introduced in Antiphonal Reading. On the following page is an example of a poem written in two parts by fourth-grade students.

The Titanic

Titanic	Titanic
	Hit an iceberg
Titanic	Titanic
Sank to the bottom of the sea	
Titanic	Titanic
Titanic	Titanic
Titanic	Titanic
	1,025 people died
700 people lived	
Titanic	Titanic
People went under water	
	To study the
Titanic	Titanic
	We want to know why
The Titanic sank	
Titanic	Titanic
Titanic	Titanic
Titanic	Titanic
	by Rebecca and Mike

Suggested Resources

Fleischman, P. (2000). *Big talk: Poems for four voices*. New York: Candlewick.

Fleischman, P. (1988). *Joyful noise: Poems for two voices*. New York: Harper & Row.

Fleischman, P. (1989). *I am phoenix: Poems for two voices*. New York: Harper & Row.

Hoberman, M.A. (2001). *You read to me, I'll read to you: Very short stories to read together*. Boston: Little, Brown.

Readers Theater

DESCRIPTION

Readers Theater is a presentation of text read aloud expressively and dramatically by two or more readers (Young & Vardell, 1993). Meaning is conveyed to the audience, primarily through readers' expressive and interpretive readings rather than through actions, costumes, or props. Students can read from commercially-prepared scripts or develop scripts from materials they are reading, either narrative or expository in nature. General characteristics of Readers Theater include: no full memorization; holding scripts during the performance; no full costumes or staging; and narration providing a framework for the dramatic action conveyed by the readers. The primary aim of Readers Theater is to promote reading (Shepard, 1997), and it appears to do so, as the practice for a Readers Theater performance gives new purpose and added enjoyment for reading stories and books repeatedly. Martinez, Roser, and Strecker (1998/1999) offered an instructional plan for developing Readers Theater with young readers using narrative text, and Roser (2001) demonstrated that Reader's Theater strategies can also help Hispanic middle-grade students learn to read in their second language of English.

PROCEDURE

1. Develop or select a script to be used with students. Such development may mean adding brief narration to describe the action in the story or dividing longer narrations into speaking parts for more than one narrator. Possible resources can be found in the box on the following page.
2. Read aloud from the story on which the script is based. Provide a good model of fluent reading.
3. Provide a brief lesson on one aspect of fluency, perhaps noting the signals in the text that might help students know how to read it aloud, or discuss how the characters might be feeling at selected points in the story. This discussion should help provide insights about how each character might sound.
4. Distribute scripts to the students and have them read silently or with a buddy. You may want to encourage students to take the scripts home for additional practice.
5. The next day, have students practice reading the script aloud again; then determine who will be reading each role for performance purposes.
6. Have students spend the next day highlighting their parts in the script and reading and rereading their assigned roles with their group. Encourage students to think about how they might best convey the feelings of the character they are representing. They should also consider other ways they can help the audience understand the story and where they will stand or sit during the performance.

7. Finally, in front of an audience consisting of parents, school personnel, or other members of the class, have students perform their Readers Theater production.
8. See Appendix B for two Readers Theater scripts.

Suggested Resources

http://www.aaronshep.com/rt

http://www.geocities.com/EnchantedForest/Tower/3235

http://www.lisablau.com/scriptomonth.html

http://loiswalker.com/catalog/guidesamples.html

http://www.readers-theatre.com

http://www.stemnet.nf.ca/CITE/langrt.htm#Gander

http://www.storycart.com

Barchers, S.I. (1993). *Readers theatre for beginning readers*. Englewood, CO: Teacher Ideas Press.

Bauer, C.F. (1991). *Presenting reader's theater: Plays and poems to read aloud*. New York: H.W. Wilson.

Blau, L. (2000). The best of reader's theater. Seattle, WA: One from the Heart.

Braun, W., & Braun, C. (2000). *A readers theatre treasury of stories*. Winnipeg, MB: Peguis.

Dixon, N., Davies, A., & Politano, C. (1996). *Learning with readers theatre*. Winnipeg, MB: Peguis.

Frederick, A., & Stoner, A. (1993). Frantic frogs and other frankly fractured folktales for readers theatre. Greenwood Village, CO: Teacher Ideas Press.

Glasscock, S. (2000). *10 American history plays for the classroom*. New York: Scholastic.

Haven, K. (1996). *Great moments in science experiments and readers theatre*. Greenwood Village, CO: Teacher Ideas Press.

Hill, S. (1990). *Readers theatre: Performing the text*. Winnipeg, MB: Peguis.

Ratliff, G.L. (1999). *Introduction to readers theatre: A classroom guide to performance*. Colorado Springs, CO: Meriwether Publishing.

Shepard, A. (1993). *Stories on stage: Scripts for reader's theater*. New York: H.W. Wilson.

Walker, L. (1997). *Readers theatre strategies for the middle and junior high classroom*. Colorado Springs, CO: Meriwether Publishing.

Radio Reading

DESCRIPTION

Radio Reading provides an opportunity for students to use their experiences with audio-only technology to model fluent reading and communicate a message to their peers (Greene, 1979; Searfoss, 1975). In Radio Reading, students read fluently for the purpose of performing and sharing a selected portion of text with others. Just as radio announcers do, they must read with expression at a comprehensible rate so that the listener can focus on the meaning and possible enjoyment of the passage. The procedure has four components: 1) getting started, 2) communicating the message, 3) checking for understanding, and 4) clarifying an unclear message (Searfoss, 1975). Opitz and Rasinski (1998) adapted the original procedure to allow students to practice preselected text prior to reading it aloud. For each portion of the text, one student assumes the role of the radio announcer, and the other students assume the roles of the radio listeners, just as they would when listening to an actual radio broadcast. Only the reader and the teacher have copies of the text open during the reading. All other students are active listeners with books closed. Allowing the reader to hold a microphone or use a toy karaoke machine should enhance the fun and increase motivation.

PROCEDURE

1. Select material that is at the student's instructional level. Materials at the student's instructional level are typically read with 95% accuracy.
2. On the day preceding the Radio Reading experience, explain the procedure to students. Emphasize that it is the reader's responsibility to communicate a message, much like a radio announcer does. Assign segments of text to students to prepare for the next day. These segments might be from a basal story the group has read, from a trade book or chapter book, from content area material, or from a student periodical.
3. Provide opportunities for students to practice their segments. This practice might be done with a buddy at school or with a parent or sibling at home.
4. In addition to practicing the selection, invite each student to prepare a question or two about the material that can be posed to the listeners following the reading. The questions might be literal or more open-ended, leading to discussion possibilities.

5. On the day you use Radio Reading, review with students the procedures listed below (and summarized on the following page) before beginning the session.

- The reader reads the assigned passage aloud with meaning and expression.
- If the reader miscalls a word, the reader is to correct it and go on reading, keeping the flow of the reading, and thus the meaning, intact.
- If the reader hesitates and can't quickly say a word, the reader may ask the teacher, "What is that word?" The teacher should immediately supply the word, thus preserving the message of the passage for listeners. If the reader hesitates and does not ask for help, the teacher waits a predetermined amount of time for the reader to supply the word (perhaps 5 seconds) and then tells the student the word.
- When the first student has finished reading, the questions he or she has prepared may be asked of the listeners right away or postponed until all of the reading has been completed. Listeners could also be asked to provide a quick summary of what they heard.
- If a reader has not communicated the message of the passage clearly or there is some confusion on the part of the listeners, then the reader is asked to reread the portion of text to help clarify and correct the confusion.
- Additional students then take turns reading their text segments for the listeners.

6. At the conclusion of the Radio Reading experience, each student then poses his or her questions to the group if they haven't already done so, or you may lead a brief discussion about the entire text. At this time, it may also be appropriate to reflect on the elements of effective read-alouds and how the group did in modeling them during the day's lesson.

Procedure for Radio Reading

1. Read your selection aloud with meaning and expression.

2. If you have trouble with a word:

    •   correct it and go on.

    •   ask, "What is that word?"

3. After reading:

    •   ask the questions you have prepared for your selection.

    •   ask someone to tell what your selection was mainly about.

    •   reread portions of text to clarify and correct confusions.

Oral Recitation Lesson

DESCRIPTION

The Oral Recitation Lesson is a structured process that involves both direct and indirect instruction using narrative text (Hoffman, 1987). The lesson includes the modeling of effective oral reading and both guided and independent practice. Reutzel and Hollingsworth (1993) and Reutzel, Hollingsworth, and Eldredge (1994) found that the Oral Recitation Lesson improves both fluency and reading comprehension.

PROCEDURE

1. Read a story aloud to students.
2. Following the reading, elicit the major story elements, including setting, characters, major events, and solution. Individually or as a group, complete a story map graphic organizer. See page 41 for one example of a reproducible story map.
3. Using the story map as a guide, help students write a summary of the story. For students with little experience in summary writing, model how to write a summary using the information from the story map. For students who are more familiar with summary writing, you might use shared or interactive writing to complete the story summary. More advanced or more able students may be able to complete the summary independently.
4. Following the completion of the story map and summary, read aloud a selected portion of the story, perhaps one that was particularly exciting, meaningful, or eventful.
5. After reading the segment of the text aloud, have students read it chorally (see page 32) with you until they appear to be reading with good rate, accuracy, and expression.
6. Next, put students into pairs and have them read the story segment to each other. Ask students to read the passage just as you have practiced it together. Remind students that effective oral reading involves reading like they are talking, with accuracy and expression, for the purpose of communicating understanding.
7. When students have completed the partner reading, read aloud another portion of the text and follow it with Choral Reading (see page 32) and partner reading, until several segments of the text have been modeled and practiced.
8. On another day, ask students to select one of the modeled and practiced passages and read it aloud to a peer group. Following each reading, ask listeners to make one or two positive comments about each reader's performance.
9. On successive days (usually two to four), ask students to read aloud in a soft voice to themselves for about ten minutes, using the same passages previously practiced. Move around the class or group and listen to students as they read, providing feedback as appropriate.

Story Map

Name _____ Date _____

Title

Setting

Characters

Problem

Events

⇩

⇩

⇩

Solution

Based on Beck and McKeown (1981).

Fluency
Development Lesson

DESCRIPTION

The Fluency Development Lesson combines several oral reading strategies to create multiple opportunities for readers who struggle to hear and practice fluent reading (Rasinski & Padak, 1996). The lesson is designed to be used at least four times per week over an extended period of time, to encourage accurate word recognition and expression which ultimately contribute to thoughtful reading. This procedure involves reading to, with, and by students.

PROCEDURE

1. Give students copies of a reading passage consisting of 50 to 200 words.
2. Read the text aloud while students follow along silently. This step may be repeated several times.
3. Discuss the content of the text with the students and encourage them to think about the way in which you read it aloud to them. Ask them how you used your voice, rate, and expression to help convey the meaning of the text.
4. Next, using Echo Reading (see page 31) and then Choral Reading (see page 32), have students read the text with you. It is important to continue to model fluent reading as students read with you and echo your reading.
5. When students appear to be developing proficiency and confidence in reading the text with you, have students form pairs.
6. Have student pairs move to various locations in the classroom. One student now reads the text aloud three times to his or her partner, while the partner follows along in the text. The listener provides help, if needed, and gives positive feedback such as, "You read all the words correctly," or "You really sounded excited when you read the part where they were running away from the bear."
7. Have students reverse their roles so the reader becomes the listener and the listener becomes the reader. Repeat the above step.
8. Ask students to come back together as a whole group and ask for volunteers to read the text aloud to the entire group. At this time, the listeners do not follow along, but instead, enjoy the performance of their peers.
9. Praise students for their oral reading proficiency and their excellent listening behaviors.
10. Encourage students to take one copy of the passage home and read it to parents and relatives.
11. Put one copy of the passage into a notebook or folder for each student. Selected passages can be used for choral reading on successive days.

Say It Like the Character

DESCRIPTION

Say It Like the Character helps students learn to make inferences as they become more fluent readers (Opitz & Rasinski, 1998). When students read silently, they may not think about the way a character feels or how the character might speak. In Say It Like the Character, students are developing prosody as they are asked to read aloud using the intonation and expression they believe the character in the story might use when speaking. Thus, the story becomes more meaningful, and interpretations about the character are elicited.

PROCEDURE

1. Ask students to read a given text silently. Be sure the selection contains character dialogue.
2. Select a segment of the text and ask students to reread it silently, thinking about how the character(s) might sound when speaking.
3. Invite a student or students to read the segment aloud in the way the character(s) might actually speak, thus conveying the feelings of the character(s) to the listener. You might use some of the following questions:

   - What emotion(s) were you conveying as you read to us?
   - What made you decide to read as you did?
   - Did you connect something in your own experience with that of the character(s)? If so, what?
   - Were there any typographic signals in the text that helped you know how to use your voice, for instance, large, bold type or exclamation marks?

4. As students continue reading silently, encourage them to pay attention to the events in the story, the typographical signals the author gives, and the ways the author helps the reader understand the characters and their feelings.
5. As a follow-up activity, you may wish to do the following:

   - Have students share the signals in the selection that they used to "say it like the character."
   - Select sentences from the text and print them on sentence strips. For example,

     "What is that crazy horse doing?" people asked one another.

     The ducks marched right out of the park in a straight line.

     Night came, and the lights went on in the city.

     "But wait! We need to get the camera."

Waving his arms frantically, he shouted at the driver to stop.

We worked side by side . . . long into the night.

"Dress warmly, Jenny," her mom called.

She swallowed hard, "I've learned a lot this summer."

- Print words that convey specific emotions on index cards. Some example words might be *fear*, *excitement*, *joy*, and *anger*.
- Invite students to choose one emotion card and one sentence strip and then read the sentence aloud, conveying the emotion on the card. Listeners might be invited to guess the emotion being expressed by the reader, thus turning it into a game and enhancing motivation for fluency practice (Person, 1993).

Super Signals

DESCRIPTION

Super Signals involves helping students look for and understand the typographic signals that are used to help convey the author's message. Signals such as bold or italic type, commas, exclamation marks, and type size are often clues to meaning that should be noted by the reader, particularly during oral reading.

PROCEDURE

1. Select a text that contains signals you wish to help students understand, for example, bold or enlarged type, exclamation marks, or italicized type.
2. Use a big book or enlarge the passage for use on an overhead projector.
3. Read the selection aloud to the students, allowing them to see the text as you read. During the first reading, use no expression, pauses, or changes in pitch.
4. Reread the same passage aloud, using differing pitches, pauses, and expression as indicated by the text.
5. Discuss with students the differences in the two readings. Encourage them to explain why you changed your reading the second time. Ask them which reading helped them better understand the text.
6. Encourage students to note the signals in the text that helped you know when to pause, raise your voice, or stop. Note how using these signals enhances understanding of the text.
7. Provide students with text that contains some of the Super Signals you have just modeled. Ask them to first read it silently and then to read it aloud, showing that they understand the signals.
8. Tell students to look for Super Signals in their reading and use these important clues to gain the author's meaning.
9. You may wish to create a classroom chart of Super Signals. Invite students to share Super Signals that they locate in their reading materials and note how these signals are used to convey meaning (Opitz & Rasinski, 1998). A sample chart is shown on the following page.

OUR SUPER SIGNALS CHART

Super Signal	What It Means	Example
Exclamation Mark	Excitement	"Think! Think!"
Italics	Emphasis	"But I want *more*! And I want *you* to make it for me!" "Where did you get *this*?" he asked, showing her the gold.
Dash	Pause	"You don't need them anymore—your people love you now."
Comma	Pause Cluster words between commas together as you read them.	And whenever the king started worrying about gold, she sent him on a goodwill trip throughout the countryside, which cheered him up.

Phrase Boundaries

DESCRIPTION

One aspect of fluency involves clustering reading into appropriate phrases, rather than reading word by word. Appropriate phrasing helps the reader to understand the passage (Shanahan, 2000b). Cromer (1970) and O'Shea and Sindelar (1983) found that using text segmented into phrasal units resulted in improved comprehension, particularly for students who may be slow, but accurate, readers. Teaching students to read in phrases involves modeling appropriate phrasing, giving students guided practice in phrasing, and then moving toward independent practice in proper phrasing. Finally, students are invited to work with new materials to decide where phrase boundaries should be placed in order to enhance comprehension of the text. Rasinski (1990) found that the practice of marking phrase boundaries can lead to improved oral reading performance and comprehension, particularly for less able students.

PROCEDURE

1. Provide copies of a phrase-cued text that has boundaries marked with a slash mark "/," or show the marked text on the overhead projector. You might wish to use one slash mark for phrases within a sentence and double slash marks at the end of a sentence. For example, "The ducks/ marched out of the park/ in a straight line."// or "Waving his arms frantically,/ he shouted at the driver to stop."//

2. Read the text aloud to students, demonstrating how you group the words together in each of the phrases.

3. Invite students to read the text aloud with you, grouping the words just as you have modeled.

4. After students appear to be successfully reading the text in phrases with you, have them read the text aloud individually or in pairs, remembering to continue to read in phrases.

5. On another day, give students copies of the material that has been practiced. Ask them to add slash marks to indicate the phrase boundaries. Have students check their phrasing by reading aloud to each other or to you. Their phrasing should be meaningful and should demonstrate comprehension of the passage.

6. When students appear to become more proficient at reading in phrases, provide copies of new materials to students. Ask them to read the materials and mark the phrase boundaries independently. To check the accuracy of their markings, have one or two students read aloud, using the phrases they have created. Allow students in the class to decide if the phrasing enhances comprehension. Shanahan (2000b) suggests that independent marking of such boundaries can be given as a homework assignment to older students.

Assisted Reading

Paired Reading   49

Neurological Impress Method   52

Preview-Pause-Prompt-Praise   53

Structured Repeated Readings   56

Tape, Check, Chart   59

Reading While Listening   61

Paired Reading

DESCRIPTION

Paired Reading, originally developed for use by parents and their children, is also a useful technique in the classroom (Topping, 1987a, 1987b, 1989). The tutor, a more capable reader, supports the tutee in reading materials that are generally more difficult than those read independently. In addition to supplying support in word recognition, the tutor also plays a major role in extending understanding of the text through discussion and questioning. Paired Reading has been found effective in improving accuracy and comprehension for students of all abilities between the ages of 6 and 13 (Topping, 1987a). The procedure for Paired Reading is easy to learn and implement in the classroom. Topping (1989) recommends that pairs work together three times per week for a minimum of six weeks, in sessions ranging from 15 to 30 minutes.

PROCEDURE

1. Allow the tutee to select reading material within his or her instructional level.
2. Choose a comfortable place to read where both you and the tutee can see the text easily.
3. Begin by reading the text chorally (see page 32) at a speed that is comfortable for the tutee. If the tutee makes an error, say the word correctly. Have the tutee repeat the word and then proceed with choral reading. For example, if the tutee says "second" for "secret" in the sentence, "Gary promised to keep everything a secret," the tutor would stop reading and say "secret." The tutee would repeat the word "secret," and the pair would continue reading chorally.
4. If the tutee self-corrects a miscue, offer praise. Also praise the tutee if other self-monitoring behaviors are exhibited and for using good rate and prosody (stress, pitch, and phrasing).
5. If the text selected is at the tutee's independent reading level, the tutee can choose to read it aloud without the support of the tutor. When the tutee uses a prearranged signal (e.g., a tap or nudge), stop reading chorally with the tutee.
6. If the tutee encounters a difficult word, wait for five seconds. If the tutee does not correctly read the word, provide the word and return to reading chorally with the tutee.
7. Continue reading chorally until the tutee again signals that he or she wishes to read without support.
8. At the completion of the session, talk with the tutee about reading behaviors that are improving. Note progress on the Paired Reading Record Sheet (see page 50) and/or on the sheet titled How Well Did Your Partner Read? (see page 51).

Paired Reading Record Sheet

Tutor_____ Tutee_____

Date	Material Read	Behaviors Noted	Minutes of Reading (Circle One)
			5 10 15 20 25 30
			5 10 15 20 25 30
			5 10 15 20 25 30
			5 10 15 20 25 30
			5 10 15 20 25 30

How Well Did Your Partner Read?

Tutor _____ Tutee _____

What We Read _____ Date _____

Check (✓) what your partner did while reading.

_____ Read Smoothly   _____ Read Quickly

_____ Knew Most Words   _____ Used Punctuation Correctly

_____ Used Good Expression   _____ Sounded Like Talking

Tell your partner one thing that was better about his or her reading.

Have your partner circle the word or words that tells how well he or she thinks the reading went.

Terrible   Not So Good   OK   Good   Great

Choose one thing to work on next time you read together and write it below.

_____

Comments:

_____

_____

_____

Neurological Impress Method

DESCRIPTION

The Neurological Impress Method involves the teacher and the student reading aloud simultaneously from the same book (Heckelman, 1969). The teacher reads slightly faster than the student to keep the reading fluent. The teacher usually sits next to the student and focuses his or her voice near the ear of the student. The goal is to help the student engage in a fluent reading experience. This method offers some of the guidance mentioned by the National Reading Panel (2000).

PROCEDURE

1. Select an interesting book or passage that is appropriate for the student's reading level. It is recommended that you begin with easy reading materials that the student can read with at least 95% accuracy. You might want the student to choose materials from among several appropriate preselected items.

2. Relate the need to practice reading to some activity in which the student participates (e.g., soccer, swimming, or art). Stress that practice is necessary to excel in many activities, such as sports and reading. Tell the student that you will help the student practice by reading with him or her.

3. Have the student sit slightly in front of you so that your voice is close to the student's ear. Begin by reading the selected material out loud together. You should read a *little* louder and faster than the student.

4. Run your finger under the words simultaneously as the words are read. Have the student assume this task when he or she is confident enough. Make sure that print, finger, and voice operate together. You may want to assist the student by placing your hand over the student's and guiding it smoothly.

5. Reread the initial lines or paragraph several times together to build confidence and comfort with the method before proceeding to new material. As the passage is reread, drop your voice behind the student's, if you think he or she is gaining fluency.

6. Read for two to three minutes in the initial sessions. The goal should be to establish a fluent reading pattern. Appropriate intonation and expression in reading are vital. The major concern is with the style of the reading.

7. Supplement the Neurological Impress Method with Echo Reading (see page 31) if the student has extreme difficulty with saying a word or phrase. Say the phrase and have the student repeat the phrase. When the student has satisfactorily repeated the phrase several times, return to the book or passage.

8. From time to time, speed up the pace for just a few minutes. Heckelman (1969) suggests using the Neurological Impress Method daily for up to fifteen minutes to provide a total of ten hours of assistance. An alternative might be to use the method several times a week for several months. A paraprofessional or volunteer might be trained to work with individual students—especially those who struggle with reading.

Preview-Pause-Prompt-Praise

DESCRIPTION

Preview-Pause-Prompt-Praise is a peer tutoring technique used to develop self-monitoring and fluent reading (Allington, 2001; Corso, Funk, & Gaffney, 2001/2002; Topping, 1987b). Pairs of students, often of differing ages or reading abilities, read together from the same text and support each other through the reading by using the Preview-Pause-Prompt-Praise technique. Allington (2001) recommends that parents, teachers, teaching assistants, and peers use a similar strategy when listening to students read aloud.

PROCEDURE

1. Pair students with older or more able reading tutors.
2. The tutor *previews* the reading, by discussing the cover and title of the book with the reader and then posing the question, "What do you think this will be about?" Several brief ideas may be shared with reasons offered. (See Tutor Guide on page 55.)
3. The tutee then begins reading aloud while the tutor listens, or the pair may read the first few sentences together chorally. If the reading is done chorally, the tutor discontinues reading along after the first few sentences, and the tutee continues to read aloud to the tutor.
4. If the tutee miscalls a word or appears to be having difficulty, the tutor should *pause* for three to five seconds to wait for the student to self-correct or read to the end of the sentence.
5. If the reader does not make a self-correction, decode the word, or reread the sentence correctly, the tutor provides *prompts* to assist the reader. For example:

   - If the word does not make sense, the tutor prompts with a clue to the meaning by saying, "Does that make sense? Does it sound right? What word would sound right?"
   - If the word makes sense, but it is incorrect, the tutor might prompt the tutee to look more carefully at the letters in the word by saying, "What does the word start with? Do you see a part of the word that you know? Can you reread, say the first sound, and see if the word falls out of your mouth?"
   - If the tutee stops, the tutor might say, "Go back to the beginning of the sentence and try reading it again."
   - If, after two prompts, the tutee still does not correct the problem, the tutor tells the tutee the word.

6. If the tutee self-corrects, or in some way fixes the problem, the tutor *praises* the tutee and invites him or her to continue reading.

7. After reading, the tutor *praises* something the tutee did well, for example, "I noticed that you stopped and went back when what you were reading didn't seem to make sense. That's something that good readers do."
8. The reading time concludes with the tutor asking, "What was your favorite part?" The tutor may also wish to share his or her favorite part as well.

Tutor Guide

Tutor_____ Name of Reader_____

Title of Selection_____ Date_____

To Begin

Preview

Look at the cover and title of the book. Ask, **"What do you think this will be about?"**

"Let's start by reading together. When I stop reading along with you, you should keep reading."

During Reading

If the reader struggles and does not fix a problem, **Pause** and
slowly count to five. Then you might **Prompt** by saying the following:

Does that make sense?

Does that look right?

Does that sound right?

After Reading

Praise

Tell the reader about something he or she did well. You might say, **"I noticed how you went back and figured out the word that you struggled with."**

Ask, **"What was your favorite part?"**

Then offer your favorite part. You might say, **"I really liked this part the best."** If your favorite part is the same one the reader chose, you might say, **"I liked that part, too!"**

Structured Repeated Readings

DESCRIPTION

The method of Structured Repeated Readings is a motivational strategy that engages students in repeated readings of text (Samuels, 1979). A Reading Progress Chart helps monitor the student's growth in fluency, which results, in part, from the automatic recognition of words and the reduction of miscues. Engaging students in repeated readings of text "is particularly effective in fostering more fluent reading" in students "struggling to develop proficient reading strategies" (Allington, 2001, p. 73). This specific instructional approach was among those mentioned by the National Reading Panel (2000) as an effective practice. The following procedure has been adapted from Johns and Lenski (2001).

PROCEDURE

1. Select a brief passage or story of 50 to 200 words for the student to read aloud. For beginning readers or readers who struggle, a passage of approximately 50 words is sufficient for the first time the strategy is used. The passage should be at an appropriate level of difficulty. That means that the student should generally recognize more than 90% of the words. If the passage contains 50 words, the student should generally recognize about 45 of the words. If the student misses more than 6 words in a 50-word passage, it is probably not suitable for use in repeated reading experiences.

2. Ask the student to read the passage orally. Using a copy of the passage, note the student's miscues and keep track of the time (in seconds) it took the student to read the passage.

3. Ask the student to tell you something about the passage or ask a question or two. Be sure that the student is not just calling words.

4. Record the time in seconds and the number of miscues as in the sample on page 57. In the example in the sidebar, the student read a 45-word passage in 58 seconds and made 4 miscues. To convert seconds into rate in words per minute (WPM), multiply the number of words in the passage by 60 and then divide by the time (in seconds) it took the student to read the passage. As noted in the example, the rate is approximately 46 words per minute (WPM).

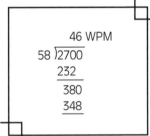

5. Encourage the student to practice rereading the passage independently for a day or two. The reading can be done both orally and silently. It can also be done at home. The goal is to have the student practice the passage several times before you next meet with the student to repeat the process described in Step 2.

6. Repeat the process of having the student read the passage to you. Record the time in seconds and the number of miscues on the chart under Reading 2. Continue this general procedure over a period of time, until a suitable rate is achieved. You can use your professional judgment to determine a suitable rate or refer to the norms for oral-reading rates provided on pages 5, 6, and 7. The chart below shows the five readings for a second-grade student over a 10-day period. The initial rate of 56 WPM was increased to approximately 87 WPM by the fifth reading. According to the norms provided for second graders in the spring of the year (see page 6), this student's rate is slightly below average.

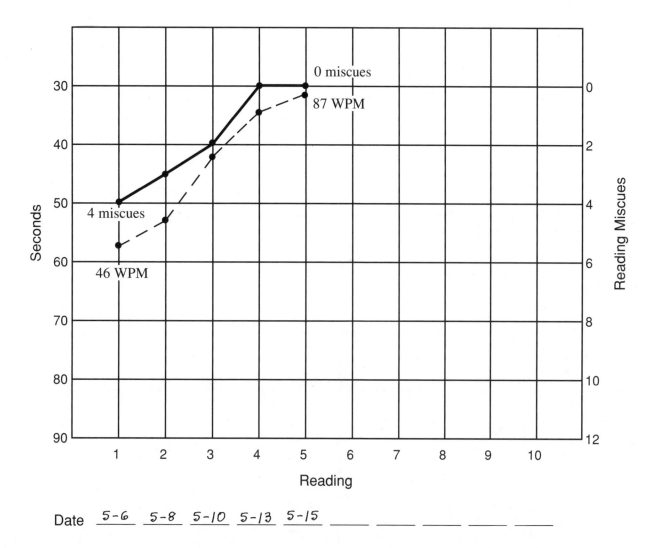

Date 5-6   5-8   5-10   5-13   5-15   ____   ____   ____   ____   ____

7. Repeat the strategy with a new selection. As you use the Reading Progress Chart on page 58, note that space is provided to record the date and to chart up to ten readings. You should base the actual number of readings on the student's progress in fluency. Some students will achieve a satisfactory level of fluency after a few readings; other students may need six or seven readings. Be flexible and responsive to individual differences. The Reading Progress Chart was designed to show visible evidence of gains. Students are encouraged as they see visible evidence of their progress and are motivated to improve their rate and accuracy. The charts can be a meaningful way to gather evidence of fluency development over time with a variety of passages. As a chart is completed for a passage, it can be placed in the student's work folder or portfolio.

Reading Progress Chart for _____

Title/Book _____

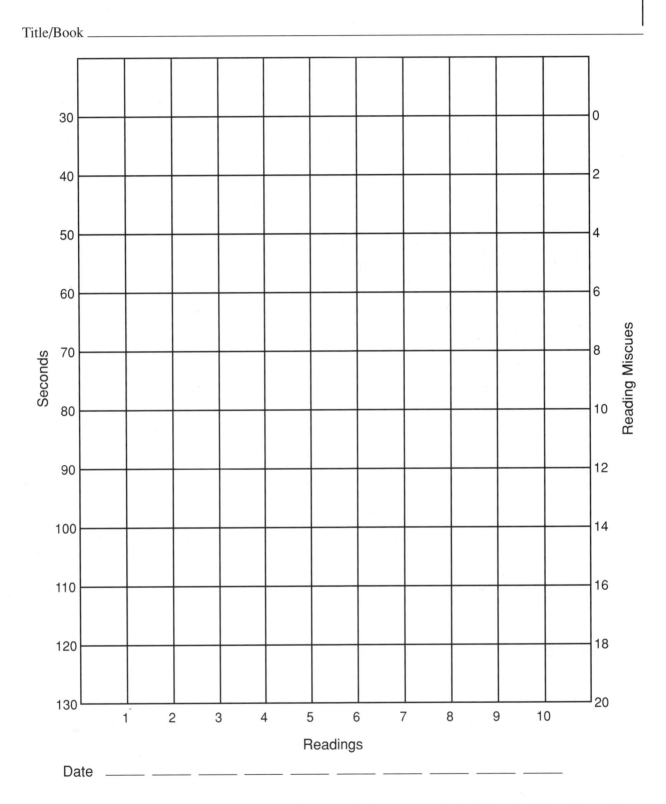

Readings

Date __ __ __ __ __ __ __ __ __ __

Tape, Check, Chart

DESCRIPTION

In this adaptation of repeated readings, students listen to audiotapes of their own reading and record their miscues. According to Allington (2001), the number of miscues generally decreases with each reading and fluency increases. In addition, having students note and chart their own progress is a visible record of their improvement and serves as an incentive to continue to work toward greater fluency.

PROCEDURE

1. Have the student read aloud a text of appropriate difficulty and record it on an audiotape. An appropriate text for repeated readings is one that the student can read with at least 90% accuracy.
2. After making the recording, have the student replay the tape and follow along in the text (or with a photocopy of the text).
3. As he or she listens to the tape recording, the student places a small check mark above each word that deviates from the text (e.g., omissions, insertions, mispronunciations).
4. Then have the student read and make another recording of the same passage. The student again notes, in a second color, any omissions, insertions, or mispronunciations with a check mark.
5. The student reads the same passage a third time, tapes the reading, listens again to the tape and marks, in a third color, the deviations from text.
6. The student then tallies and charts the number of text deviations for each reading, using the chart on page 60.
7. Meet with the student to discuss his or her progress. Give recognition for effort and progress.

Tape, Check, Chart

Name _____ Date _____

Passage _____

Recording Number	Number of Check Marks (✓)	Comments
1		
2		
3		

Name _____ Date _____

Passage _____

Recording Number	Number of Check Marks (✓)	Comments
1		
2		
3		

Name _____ Date _____

Passage _____

Recording Number	Number of Check Marks (✓)	Comments
1		
2		
3		

Reading While Listening

DESCRIPTION

In Reading While Listening (or repeated listening), students listen to recorded passages while they silently read the written version (Kuhn & Stahl, 2000). Texts with tapes or CD-ROMs are available commercially; however, in order to make the experience the most valuable, the recorded texts need to be at the students' instructional level and recorded at a speed that enables them to follow along. Cues need to be explicit (e.g., when to turn pages) to minimize students losing their places. Also, reading in phrases and having students slide their fingers under the words helps students to stay on task (Carbo, 1978, 1981). Having the teacher, teaching assistant, or parent helper prepare recordings provides the optimal opportunity for students to gain from the experience. Students who become familiar with the procedure and are fairly fluent readers can also create recordings for classroom use (Rasinski & Padak, 1996). The advantage of Reading While Listening over Structured Repeated Readings (see page 56) or the Neurological Impress Method (see page 52) is that there is much less assistance needed from the teacher, as the modeling of fluent reading is provided by the recording. This makes the procedure more usable in a classroom situation. Holding students accountable for being able to read the text fluently at the completion of several Reading While Listening sessions is critical to the success of this activity. Students know that they must practice the materials repeatedly, in order to meet the success criterion. Dowhower (1987) and Rasinski (1990) found that students made significant gains in reading speed and accuracy, and students in Carbo's study (1981) demonstrated gains in word recognition. In fact, Rasinski's study (1990) and one by Sindelar, Monda, and O'Shea (1990) found that Reading While Listening is effective for students with learning disabilities, as well as for students who represent both the the low-success and high-success range of readers in the classroom. Kuhn and Stahl (2000) caution that it is important to make a distinction between Reading While Listening and classroom listening centers. Classroom listening center experiences generally don't include holding students responsible for reading the material in a fluent manner after repeated listening experiences; therefore, students don't practice reading the material, and as a result, do not appear to make measurable gains in reading.

PROCEDURE

1. Select materials that are of interest to students and that are challenging, but not at the students' frustration level.
2. Prepare recordings of the materials, using the following guidelines:

   - Read aloud at a comfortable rate, so that students can follow along.
   - Read with good phrasing and expression.
   - Give oral or auditory signal cues to students when a page should be turned.
   - If page lay-out makes it difficult for students to know where the reading will begin, tell them explicitly on the recording where to look when following along.
   - You may wish to encourage students to finger-point to the words as they listen or use an index card or paper marker to help them keep their places.

3. Provide several copies of the text so that a small group of students may participate in the activity simultaneously.
4. Tell students that they are going to be listening to material that they will be expected to read aloud to you at a future date. Tell them that, after listening and following along several times, you will expect them to be able to read with expression, accuracy, and at a rate that sounds like they are talking.
5. Following the listening, have students practice reading the material several more times either independently and/or with a partner.
6. Finally, provide an opportunity for students to read the material aloud to you, an older student, a teaching assistant, or parent volunteer.
7. Track students' progress, paying particular attention to accuracy and rate (see Reading While Listening Program Chart on page 64). This chart has been adapted from the 5-Point Fluency Scale for Oral Reading.

Suggested Resources

Rasinski, T. *High five reading*. Mankato, MN: Capstone Curriculum (www.capstonecurriculum.com) 888-262-6135

This is a series of five books and audiocassette tapes for intermediate and middle-grade readers. The books are written on a variety of reading levels and cover a range of interest areas, including biography, sports, adventure, science, and history. The audio tapes are recorded at two speeds to enable students to listen at a rate that is comfortable for them.

Soliloquy Learning, Union City, CA
(www.soliloquylearning.com) 866-442-0920

This publisher, with the guidance of Marilyn Jager Adams, has created the Soliloquy Reading Assistant (available at www.reading-assistant.com). The CD rom uses advanced speech recognition software to provide feedback to students as they practice repeated oral readings. The most innovative feature of these materials is that the rate of reading is determined by the student rather than the software, thus enhancing the potential for fluency improvement. Reading selections are drawn from such sources as *Cricket* and *Spider* magazines and are appropriate for students in grades two through five.

Sundance Publishers, Littleton, MA
(www.sundancepub.com) 800-343-8204

This publisher has many recorded books that are unabridged sources for student listening and reading. Here are a few possibilities:

Fritz, J. *Stories of famous Americans*. Books and Cassettes (Grades 3–6)

Rey, H.A. *Curious George*. Books and Cassettes (Grades K–3)

Lobel, A. *Frog and Toad*. Books and Cassettes (Grades K–3)

Rylant, C. *Henry and Mudge*. Books and Cassettes (Grades K–3)

People to remember. Read-Along Cassettes (Grades 3 and up)

Some additional titles of talking books follow:

Dr. Seuss's ABC (1995). Living Books series. Novato, CA: Random House—Broderbund Software.

Tronic Phonics (1997). New York: Macmillan/McGraw-Hill Software.

Reading While Listening Progress Chart

Name _____

Title of Selection _____

	1	2	3	4	5
	Word-by-word	Some word-by-word, some 2–3 word phrases	Phrases; some word-by-word	Mostly in phrases	Phrasing consistently used
	Long pauses between words; struggles with words	Some hesitations; sounds out words; disrupts flow	Some smooth, some choppy phrasing	Generally smooth; may exhibit difficulty with some words	Generally smooth; good use of self-corrections
	Reads in monotone	Reads mostly in monotone	Combines use of expression with monotone	Appropriate expression used throughout much of the piece	Appropriate expression; intonation maintained throughout
	Little evidence of use of punctuation	Shows some use of punctuation	Shows some use of punctuation, but still ignores some	Use of punctuation is generally good	Uses punctuation consistently

Reading	Date	Time (in seconds)	Number of Miscues	Expression Score
1				
2				
3				
4				
5				

Independent Practice

Sustained Silent Reading (SSR)   66

Read and Relax   69

Sustained Silent Reading (SSR)

DESCRIPTION

Sustained Silent Reading (SSR) encourages students to practice self-selected materials during a designated time in the school day (Berglund & Johns, 1983; Hunt, 1970). The purpose of Sustained Silent Reading is to provide an opportunity for students to practice reading text that is relatively easy and of interest to them. The goal is to provide an opportunity for students to develop fluency and, at the same time, expand their vocabularies and develop broader knowledge of written language (Gillet & Temple, 2000). Allington (1983b) found that students do very little reading outside of school. This contributes to Stanovich's "Matthew effects" (1986), which suggests that those who read more tend to continue to become better readers, while those who read less, especially poorer readers, tend not to choose to read and, therefore, fall farther and farther behind. Sustained Silent Reading provides an opportunity for all students to build fluency in their reading through regular opportunities to practice (Pearson & Fielding, 1991).

PROCEDURE

1. Tell students that they will be having an opportunity to choose something that they would like to read and to read it for a specified period of time. Provide an opportunity for students to locate the materials and have them ready for the SSR period.
2. Designate a specific time during the day when all students will participate in SSR.
3. Go over the procedures and guidelines so that students understand expectations during this time. See page 68 for some suggested Rules for SSR Time, adapted from Anderson (2000). A useful handbook for organizing and managing an SSR program has been prepared by Pilgreen (2000).
4. Start with a short period of time, especially for young or less able students. Expand the time as students appear ready. When students ask if they can continue reading after the time is up, consider that a signal to increase your SSR time.
5. Provide materials for students who can't find something to read or who run short of materials before the time is up.
6. Be a model of good reading during SSR time. Students will be interested in what you are reading and will grow to understand that adults, as well as students, choose to read for pleasure both in and out of school.

7. Following the SSR period, compliment students on their behavior and their consideration of others during the reading time. You also may invite students to comment on their reading, if they wish. Comments may lead to extended enjoyment and to spontaneous sharing of text segments, thus promoting meaningful and positive practice in fluency and creating desire in others to read the same materials at another time.

Rules for SSR Time

- Choose more to read than you think you will need.

- Have your materials ready before SSR time begins.

- If needed, get a drink and take a restroom break before SSR time begins.

- Find a comfortable place to read and stay there during SSR time.

- Keep your hands and feet to yourself. Stretch your arms out and be sure you cannot touch anyone else from where you are sitting in your reading place. If you can touch someone, move before you begin to read.

- Keep reading. Don't notice anything else while you are reading. The only exceptions are a fire drill, disaster drill, a call to the office, or instructions from your teacher.

- Stay quiet. Noise of any kind disturbs others and prevents you and them from reading.

Read and Relax

DESCRIPTION

Read and Relax is an adaptation of Sustained Silent Reading (see page 66) developed for use in primary-grade classrooms (Maro, 2001). Similar to Sustained Silent Reading, all students read silently for a given amount of time each day. The major difference between Sustained Silent Reading and Read and Relax is that Read and Relax requires students to read materials that are at their independent reading levels—text that can be read with 99% accuracy in word recognition and 90% comprehension (Betts, 1946; Johns, 2001). Another difference is that the teacher uses think-alouds to help students understand how to select materials and use metacognitive strategies when reading independently. Also in Read and Relax, the teacher monitors students' reading by asking students to read portions of the text aloud to the teacher. The opportunity for students to self-select materials and read them for an uninterrupted period of time increases the number of words read and also increases students' involvement in the reading process. Through the process of reading many easy books, students become more fluent readers and gain competence and confidence (Gillet & Temple, 2000).

PROCEDURE

1. A well-supplied classroom library that contains materials at a wide variety of levels is essential to Read and Relax.
2. Gather a few books from the classroom library and model a Read and Relax session for your students. Gather students around you and explain that you are going to show them what Read and Relax looks like so that they will know what to do when it is their turn to Read and Relax.
3. Explain to students that while they will read their selections silently—you are going to read aloud to show them what you expect them to do as they read.
4. Open your first book and make a prediction about its content. Begin to read aloud and reflect on your predictions, making your thinking apparent to your students. Continue to read aloud, sharing your reading and your thinking as you read. You may want to show students how you ask questions and make connections as you read. For example, when reading a book about cats, you might say, "My cat falls asleep after she eats, just like the cat in this story. I wonder if cats need a special place to sleep or if they just fall asleep anywhere. Maybe I will find out as I continue to read this book."

5. In order to demonstrate what to do when a book is too difficult, struggle with some words in one of your Read and Relax books. After struggling with several words, tell your students that you can't relax with this book; therefore, it is too difficult for your Read and Relax time. Put it down and begin to read another book, modeling fluent reading. Explain that with an easy book, you can say almost all of the words and understand the story. Tell students that they should read easy books during their Read and Relax time.

6. On another day, invite students to select books and get ready for Read and Relax time. Remind them of the rules for Read and Relax, such as no talking to other students and always having several books ready to read. You may wish to post the rules so students can refer to them as needed.

7. Once Read and Relax has begun and students appear to be able to follow the behavioral guidelines, you may then begin to monitor students as they are reading. Quietly stop by students' desks and ask individual students to read some of their books to you. If the student is struggling when reading and doesn't sound relaxed, encourage the student to find an easier, more suitable, text.

Rules for Read and Relax

- Find books that are easy for you to read by yourself.

- Have your books ready for Read and Relax time.

- If you need to, get a drink and go to the bathroom before Read and Relax begins.

- Keep your hands and feet to yourself.

- Keep reading. Stop only when your teacher tells you to.

- Stay quiet.

Appendices

A—Answers to Anticipation Guide for Fluency   75
B—Scripts for Readers Theater   77

Appendix A

Answers to Anticipation Guide for Fluency

DIRECTIONS

Compare our notes to your initial impressions on the Anticipation Guide on page 2.

	T or F	AFTER READING Page(s)	AFTER READING Question(s)
1. Fluency in reading is most relevant at the beginning stages of reading.	F	3, 4, 5, 14	2, 3, 5, 8
2. Fluency is independent of comprehension.	F	3	1
3. Research has identified several methods to increase reading fluency.	T	15, 16	9, 10
4. Oral reading fluency is developed best through independent reading.	F	15	9
5. One aspect of fluency can be judged by determining the student's rate of reading in words per minute (WPM).	T	4, 7	4, 6
6. It is appropriate to consider fluency in silent reading.	T	3, 4	1, 3
7. Fluency is actually speed of reading.	F	3	1
8. Fluency strategies are primarily for students experiencing difficulty in reading.	F	16	11
9. Students should adjust reading rate according to their purposes for reading.	T	3, 4	2, 3
10. A reasonable oral fluency rate for third-grade students is 160 words per minute (WPM) by the end of the school year.	F	6	5
11. Round robin oral reading is an effective fluency activity.	F	10	7

Appendix B

Scripts for Readers Theater

The Grasshopper and the Ants   78

Moira's Birthday   81

The Grasshopper and the Ants

READERS THEATER VERSION

Reader parts: 1 Narrator, 10 solo reader parts, a small group of Ants, 1 Grasshopper, and a chorus of ALL

READER 1

1) There once was a grasshopper

READER 2

2) Who was in a party mood

READER 3

3) She sang away the summer days

READERS 1, 2, 3

4) And ate up all her food!

GRASSHOPPER

5) Oh, yes I did it, yes I did

6) I ate up all my food!

ALL

7) Hey grasshopper Gal!

8) Hate to burst your bubble

9) There's a moral to this tale

10) YOU'RE headed straight for trouble!

NARRATOR

11) When winter came she realized

12) She'd made a big mistake

13) She hadn't saved a thing to eat

14) And how her tummy ached

GRASSHOPPER

15) I haven't saved a thing to eat

16) And now my tummy aches!

http://www.scriptsforschools.com/ALL_SCRIPTS/
FREE_TEACHER_AIDES_/Sample_Read-Aloud_Scripts/

ALL

17) Hey grasshopper Gal!

18) Hate to burst your bubble

19) There's a moral to this tale

20) YOU'RE headed straight for trouble!

READER 4

21) The ants who lived next door to her

22) Had planned ahead, in fact

READER 6

23) Had worked throughout the summer heat

READERS 4, 5, 6

24) To store up food out back

GROUP OF ANTS

25) Did you ever, did you ever

26) Meet a group of ants so clever?

ALL

27) Hey grasshopper Gal!

28) Hate to burst your bubble

29) There's a moral to this tale

30) YOU'RE headed straight for trouble!

NARRATOR

31) And when our dear grasshopper

32) Came begging for some bread

33) The ants just shook their heads and said

GROUP OF ANTS

34) "You're going to end up dead!!"

ALL

35) Hey grasshopper Gal!

36) Hate to burst your bubble

37) There's a moral to this tale

38) YOU'RE headed straight for trouble!

http://www.scriptsforschools.com/ALL_SCRIPTS/
FREE_TEACHER_AIDES_/Sample_Read-Aloud_Scripts/

GRASSHOPPER

39) O.K., O.K., I've heard enough!

40) So what's the moral? Tell me please!

READER 7

41) I bet the moral's full of DON'TS!

READER 8

42) Don't sing away the summer?

READER 9

43) Don't party 'til you're fed?

READER 10

44) Don't waste your days just having fun?

READERS 7, 8, 9, 10

45) Don't lounge around in bed?

NARRATOR

46) The moral of this story is:

ALL

47) IT'S SMART TO PLAN AHEAD!

Moira's Birthday

(based upon the original book by Robert Munsch)

A Reader's Theater Script by Stephen Kohner

Moira's birthday is approaching and her parents allow her to invite only six children to her birthday party. Moira has her own ideas and before you know it, Grade One, Grade Two, Grade Three, Grade Four, Grade Five, Grade Six, and Kindergarten are all invited. "No problem!" thinks Moira.

CHARACTERS (in order of appearance):

- Narrator
- Moira
- Mom
- Dad
- Friend #1
- Friends
- Pizza Lady
- Baker

Narrator:	Ever had a fabulous birthday party? This story is about Moira who threw the biggest party of the year!
Moira:	Mom. . . . my birthday is next week. I want to invite a few people to my party.
Mom:	A few people? How many is a few?
Moira:	Just grade 1, grade 2, grade 3, grade 4, grade 5, grade 6 AAAAANNDD Kindergarten.
Mom:	You've got to be joking! You're crazy! No way José!
Narrator:	So Moira did what most kids would do in her situation. She asked her Dad.
Moira:	My birthday is next week. I want to invite some people to my party. Mom said I should ask you.
Dad:	A few people? How many is a few?
Moira:	Just grade 1, grade 2, grade 3, grade 4, grade 5, grade 6 AAAAANNDD Kindergarten.
Dad:	That's impossible! What are you thinking of? You can invite SIX kids. 1-2-3-4-5-6 and NNNNNOO Pip-Squeaks.

http://www.qesnrecit.qc.ca/schools/bchs/rtheatre/sample.htm

Moira:	Six kids. I understand. 1-2-3-4-5-6 and NNNNNOO Pip-Squeaks.
Dad:	Go and write out your invitations.
Narrator:	Moira spent the rest of the evening writing her invitations out. The next morning she went to school and handed them out. One of her best friends had not been invited.
Friend #1:	Moira, can I please, pretty please, come to your birthday party? One more person won't make a difference. PLLEEEASE!
Moira:	I guess one more can't hurt but don't tell anyone else.
Friend #1:	Okay. I promise not to tell anyone else and a promise is a promise.
Moira:	I know I can trust you. That's what friends are for.
Narrator:	By the end of the school day, Moira had invited ALL of grade 1, grade 2, grade 3, grade 4, grade 5, grade 6 AAAAANNDD Mrs. Thibault's entire Kindergarten class. She didn't dare tell her parents. Maybe they would be just a tiny bit upset. Her party was the next day. (knock at the door)
Friends:	SURPRISE! HAPPY BIRTHDAY!
Moira:	Welcome! Welcome to my party. Come in, come in! It's going to be so much fun! (friends all walk in)
Father:	Six friends. That's good. One, two, three, four, five, six. Six . . . six is the best number. LET'S PARTY!
Moira:	Maybe we should wait another minute.
Narrator:	Just then, something banged on the door like this:
All:	Bam! Bam! Bam! Bam!
Narrator:	The door burst open.
Friends:	SURPRISE! We're here! Let's party!
Moira:	What a surprise! What are you all doing here?
Narrator:	Before they could answer, they all ran in. They ran right over the father and the mother. There were kids everywhere. Kids in the bedroom, kids in the bathroom, kids in the kitchen, kids in the basement, and kids hanging off the roof!
Father:	What's going on here? There are more than six kids here!
Mother:	Who invited them all? There's more kids here than at Walt Disney World!

http://www.qesnrecit.qc.ca/schools/bchs/rtheatre/sample.htm

Mother and Father:	What are all these kids going to eat?!
Moira:	Don't Worry . . . Be Happy! I have a plan.
Narrator:	And with that Moira went to the phone and dialed 296-8080.
Moira:	Yes, this is an emergency situation. I need 200 all-dressed pizzas delivered to my home. I need them delivered NOW!
Pizza Lady:	200 pizzas??? Are you nuts? That's too many!
Moira:	Send us as many as you can. Or maybe you'd like us to come to your restaurant?
Pizza Lady:	No! No! Stay right where you are. Don't move. It will be our pleasure to deliver them right to your house—no charge! We'll send ten pizzas right away!
Narrator:	Moira then phoned up the local baker. What's a birthday party without birthday cake?
Moira:	Yes, this is Moira. I need 200 of your best birthday cakes right away!
Baker:	200 birthday cakes? Are you nuts? I can't make 200 cakes!
Moira:	I have hundreds of hungry kids over at my place all screaming for cake. Do you want us to come over and help you bake them? I'm sure we could help you out!
Baker:	No! No! Stay right where you are. Don't move. It will be our pleasure to deliver them right to your house—no charge! We'll send ten cakes right away!
Narrator:	Well, the next thing you know, a monstrous pizza delivery truck rolled into Moira's driveway. It dumped a pile of pizzas on her front lawn. Then an equally gargantuan truck drove in and dumped a pile of birthday cakes.
Moira and Friends:	FOOD! Time to eat!
Narrator:	The most amazing thing happened next. They gulped down all ten pizzas and ate up all ten birthday cakes in just ten seconds.
Moira and Friends:	MORE FOOD!
Mother:	More food? How can you eat so much? Where are we supposed to get more food from?

http://www.qesnrecit.qc.ca/schools/bchs/rtheatre/sample.htm

From Jerry L. Johns and Roberta L. Berglund, *Fluency: Questions, Answers, and Evidence-Based Strategies*. Copyright © 2002 Kendall/Hunt Publishing Company (1-800-247-3458, ext. 5). May be reproduced for noncommercial educational purposes.

Friends:	We'll find you the food. We'll be right back.
Narrator:	And with that, they all ran back to their homes. Moira and her parents waited one hour, two hours and three hours.
Mother:	I guess they're not planning to come back after all.
Father:	I guess they're not planning to come back after all.
Moira:	Just wait and see. My friends won't let me down.
Narrator:	Just then, something banged on the door like this:
All:	Bam! Bam! Bam! Bam!
Narrator:	The door burst open.
Friends:	SURPRISE! We're here! Let's party again!
Moira, Mother and Father:	Look at all this food! There's frog legs, goat cheese, dinosaur eggs, chocolate covered ants, pork liver, black beans, boiled bats, muddy mangoes and sloppy subs. This is great!
Narrator:	The kids ate and ate and ate. They ate all the food in just fifteen short minutes. Then everyone gave their presents to Moira. There were presents everywhere. Presents in the bedroom, presents in the bathroom, presents in the kitchen, presents in the basement, and presents hanging off the roof!
Moira:	Look at all these presents. There's no way I can open and use them all. It's just too much.
Mother:	Forget about the presents. Look at all this mess. There's mess all over the house. Mess in the bedroom, mess in the bathroom, mess in the kitchen, mess in the basement, and mess hanging off the roof!
Father:	And who is going to clean it up?
Moira:	Don't worry . . . Be happy! I've already thought of a plan. Listen up everybody. Whoever helps to clean up can take home a present.
Friends:	Yippee! Let's clean up!
Narrator:	In no time at all, the house was clean and the kids went home.
Mother:	Thank goodness. I'm glad that party is finished for this year!
Father:	Thank goodness. I'm glad that party is finished for this year!
Moira:	Wait . . . I think I hear another truck.

http://www.qesnrecit.qc.ca/schools/bchs/rtheatre/sample.htm

Narrator: Just then, a huge dump truck came and piled 190 all-dressed pizzas in Moira's backyard. Another truck rolled in and dumped 190 birthday cakes beside the pizzas.

Father: What are you going to do now? We can't possibly eat all this food!

Mother: There's enough food here to feed grade 1, grade 2, grade 3, grade 4, grade 5, grade 6 AAAAANNDD Mrs. Thibault's entire Kindergarten class.

Moira: You parents always worry too much. I have a solution. Tomorrow we'll just have to host another birthday party. We can invite grade 1, grade 2, grade 3, grade 4, grade 5, grade 6 AAAAANNDD Mrs. Thibault's entire Kindergarten class!

Narrator: And so that is how Moira ended up with the biggest birthday party in the entire world. Try and beat that!

http://www.qesnrecit.qc.ca/schools/bchs/rtheatre/sample.htm

References

Allington, R.L. (1983a). Fluency: The neglected reading goal. *The Reading Teacher, 36,* 556–561.

Allington, R.L. (1983b). The reading instruction provided readers of differing abilities. *Elementary School Journal, 83,* 548–559.

Allington, R.L. (2001). *What really matters for struggling readers: Designing research-based programs.* New York: Longman.

Anderson, C.A. (2000). Sustained silent reading: Try it, you'll like it. *The Reading Teacher, 54,* 258–259.

Anderson, R.C., Hiebert, E.H., Scott, J.A., & Wilkinson, I.A.G. (1985). *Becoming a nation of readers: The report of the Commission on Reading.* Washington, DC: The National Institute of Education.

Bear, D.R., & Barone, D. (1998). *Developing literacy: An integrated approach to assessment and instruction.* Boston: Houghton Mifflin.

Beck, I., & McKeown, M. (1981). Developing questions that promote comprehension: The story map. *Language Arts, 58,* 913–918.

Berglund, R.L. (1988). Shared book experience: Bridging the gap between lap reading and school reading. *Wisconsin State Reading Association Journal, 31,* 23–32.

Berglund, R.L., & Johns, J.L. (1983). A primer on uninterrupted sustained silent reading. *The Reading Teacher, 36,* 534–539.

Betts, E.A. (1946). *Foundations of reading instruction.* New York: American Book Company.

Blachowicz, C.L.Z., Sullivan, D.M., & Cieply, C. (2001). Fluency snapshots: A quick screening tool for your classroom. *Reading Psychology, 22,* 95–109.

Burns, B. (2001). *Guided reading: A how-to for all grades.* Arlington Heights, IL: SkyLight.

Burns, M.S., Griffin, P., & Snow, C.E. (Eds.) (1999). *Starting out right: A guide to promoting children's reading success.* Washington, DC: National Academy Press.

Butler, A., & Turbill, J. (1985). *Towards a reading-writing classroom.* Portsmouth, NH: Heinemann.

Carbo, M. (1978). Teaching reading with talking books. *The Reading Teacher, 32,* 267–273.

Carbo, M. (1981). Making books talk to children. *The Reading Teacher, 35,* 186–189.

Carver, R.P. (1989). Silent reading rates in grade equivalents. *Journal of Reading Behavior, 21,* 155–166.

Corso, L., Funk, S., & Gaffney, J. (2001/2002). An educational evening out. *The Reading Teacher, 55,* 326–329.

Cromer, W. (1970). The difference model: A new explanation for some reading difficulties. *Journal of Educational Psychology, 61,* 471–483.

Dowhower, S.L. (1987). Effects of repeated reading on second-grade transitional readers' fluency and comprehension. *Reading Research Quarterly, 22,* 389–406.

Dowhower, S.L. (1991). Speaking of prosody: Fluency's unattended bedfellow. *Theory Into Practice, 30,* 165–175.

Eldredge, J.L., Reutzel, D.R., & Hollingsworth, P.M. (1996). Comparing the effectiveness of two oral reading practices: Round-robin reading and the shared book experience. *Journal of Literacy Research, 28,* 201–225.

Elley, W.B. (1988). Vocabulary acquisition from listening to stories. *Reading Research Quarterly, 24,* 174–187.

Forman, J., & Sanders, M.E. (1998). *Project Leap First Grade Norming Study: 1993–1998.* Unpublished Manuscript.

Fountas, I.C., & Pinnell, G.S. (2000). *Matching books to readers: Using leveled books in guided reading, K–3.* Portsmouth, NH: Heinemann.

Fountas, I.C., & Pinnell, G.S. (2001). *Guiding readers and writers: Grades 3–6*. Portsmouth, NH: Heinemann.

Gillet, J.W., & Temple, C. (2000). *Understanding reading problems: Assessment and instruction* (5th ed.). New York: Harper Collins.

Greene, F. (1979). Radio reading. In C. Pennock (Ed.), *Reading comprehension at four linguistic levels* (pp. 104–107). Newark, DE: International Reading Association.

Harris, T.L., & Hodges, R.E. (Eds.) (1995). *The literacy dictionary: The vocabulary of reading and writing*. Newark, DE: International Reading Association.

Hasbrouck, J.E., & Tindal, G. (1992). Curriculum-based oral reading fluency norms for students in grades 2 through 5. *Teaching Exceptional Children, 24,* 41–44.

Heckelman, R.G. (1969). A neurological-impress method of remedial-reading instruction. *Academic Therapy Quarterly, 4,* 277–282.

Heilman, A.W., Blair, T.R., & Rupley, W.H. (2002). *Principles and practices of teaching reading* (10th ed.). Upper Saddle River, NJ: Merrill Prentice-Hall.

Herrell, A.L. (2000). *Fifty strategies for teaching English language learners*. Upper Saddle River, NJ: Prentice-Hall.

Hoffman, J.V. (1987). Rethinking the role of oral reading in basal instruction. *Elementary School Journal, 87,* 367–373.

Holdaway, D. (1979). *The foundations of literacy*. Portsmouth, NH: Heinemann.

Howe, K.B., & Shinn, M.M. (2001). *Standard reading assessment passages (RAPS) for use in general outcome measurement: A manual describing development and technical features*. Eden Prairie, MN: Edformation.

Hunt, L.C., Jr. (1970). The effect of self-selection, interest, and motivation on independent, instructional, and frustrational levels. *The Reading Teacher, 24,* 146–151, 158.

Hyatt, A.V. (1943). *The place of oral reading in the school program: Its history and development from 1880–1941*. New York: Teachers College Press.

International Reading Association (2000). *Making a difference means making it different: A position statement of the International Reading Association*. Newark, DE: Author.

Johns, J.L. (1975). Dolch list of common nouns—A comparison. *The Reading Teacher, 28,* 338–340.

Johns, J.L. (1976). Updating the Dolch basic sight vocabulary. *Reading Horizons, 16,* 104–111.

Johns, J.L. (2001). *Basic reading inventory* (8th ed.). Dubuque, IA: Kendall/Hunt.

Johns, J.L., & Lenski, S.D. (2001). *Improving reading: Strategies and resources* (3rd ed.). Dubuque, IA: Kendall/Hunt.

Johns, J.L., Lenski, S.D., & Elish-Piper, L. (2002). *Teaching beginning readers: Linking assessment and instruction* (2nd ed.). Dubuque, IA: Kendall/Hunt.

Johns, J.L., & Galen, N. (1977). Reading instruction in the middle 50's: What tomorrow's teachers remember today. *Reading Horizons, 17,* 251–254.

Keene, E.D., & Zimmermann, S. (1997). *Mosaic of thought*. Portsmouth, NH: Heinemann.

Klenk, L., & Kibby, M.L. (2000). Re-mediating reading difficulties: Appraising the past, reconciling the present, constructing the future. In M.L. Kamil, P.B. Mosenthal, P.D. Pearson, & R. Barr (Eds.), *Handbook of reading research* (Vol. III) (pp. 667–690). Mahwah, NJ: Erlbaum.

Kuhn, M.R., & Stahl, S.A. (2000). *Fluency: A review of developmental and remedial practices*. Ann Arbor, MI: Center for the Improvement of Early Reading Achievement.

LaBerge, D., & Samuels, S.J. (1974). Toward a theory of automatic information processing in reading. *Cognitive Psychology, 6,* 293–323.

Layne, S.L. (1996). *Vocabulary acquisition by fourth-grade students from listening to teachers' oral reading of novels*. Unpublished doctoral dissertation, Northern Illinois University, DeKalb.

Mallon, B., & Berglund, R.L. (1984). The language experience approach to reading: Recurring questions and their answers. *The Reading Teacher, 37,* 867–871.

Maro, N. (2001). Reading to improve fluency. *Illinois Reading Council Journal, 29*(3), 10–18.

Martin, B., Jr. (1987) *Brown bear, brown bear, what do you see?* New York: Holt.

Martinez, M., Roser, N.L., & Strecker, S. (1998/1999). "I never thought I could be a star:" A Readers Theatre ticket to fluency. *The Reading Teacher, 52*, 326–334.

Miccinati, J. (1985). Using prosodic cues to teach oral reading fluency. *The Reading Teacher, 39*, 206–212.

National Reading Panel (2000). *Teaching children to read: An evidenced-based assessment of the scientific research literature on reading and its implications for reading instruction.* Washington, DC: National Institute of Child Health & Human Development.

New Standards Primary Literacy Committee (1999). *Reading & writing grade by grade: Primary literacy standards for kindergarten through third grade.* Pittsburgh: National Center on Education and the Economy and the University of Pittsburgh.

Opitz, M.F., & Ford, M.P. (2001). *Reaching readers: Flexible & innovative strategies for guided reading.* Portsmouth, NH: Heinemann.

Opitz, M.F., & Rasinski, T.V. (1998). *Good-bye round robin: 25 effective oral reading strategies.* Portsmouth, NH: Heinemann.

O'Shea, L.J., & Sindelar, P.T. (1983). The effects of segmenting written discourse on the reading comprehension of low- and high-performance readers. *Reading Research Quarterly, 18*, 458–465.

Pearson, P.D., & Fielding, L. (1991). Comprehension instruction. In R. Barr, M.L. Kamil, P. Mosenthal, & P.D. Pearson (Eds.), *Handbook of reading research* (Vol. II) (pp. 815–860). New York: Longman.

Person, M.E. (1993). Say it right! In M.W. Olson & S.P. Homan, (Eds.). *Teacher to teacher: Strategies for the elementary classroom* (pp. 37–38). Newark, DE: International Reading Association.

Pilgreen, J. (2000). The SSR handbook: How to organize and manage a Sustained Silent Reading program. Portsmouth, NH: Heinemann.

Pinnell, G.S., Pikulski, J.J., Wixson, K.K., Campbell, J.R., Gough, P.B., & Beatty, A.S. (1995). *Listening to children read aloud.* Washington, DC: Office of Educational Research and Improvement, U.S. Department of Education.

Rasinski, T.V. (1990). Effects of repeated reading and listening-while-reading on reading fluency. *Journal of Educational Research, 83*, 147–150.

Rasinski, T., & Padak, N. (1996). *Holistic reading strategies: Teaching students who find reading difficult.* Englewood Cliffs, NJ: Merrill.

Reutzel, D.R., & Hollingsworth, P.M. (1993). Effects of fluency training on second graders' reading comprehension. *Journal of Educational Research, 86*, 325–331.

Reutzel, D.R., Hollingsworth, P.M., & Eldredge, L. (1994). Oral reading instruction: The impact on student reading comprehension. *Journal of Educational Research, 86*, 325–331.

Roser, N.L. (2001). *Supporting the literacy of bilingual middle graders with culturally relevant readers theatre scripts.* Paper presented at the 46th Annual Convention of the International Reading Association, New Orleans, LA.

Samuels, S.J. (1979). The method of repeated readings. *The Reading Teacher, 32*, 403–408.

Searfoss, L. (1975). Radio reading. *The Reading Teacher, 29*, 295–296.

Shanahan, T. (2000a). *Literacy teaching framework.* Unpublished manuscript, University of Illinois at Chicago.

Shanahan, T. (2000b). *Teaching fluency in the high school.* Unpublished manuscript, University of Illinois at Chicago.

Shepard, A. (1997). *From stories to stage: Tips for reader's theatre.* http://www.aaronshep.com/rt/Tips3

Sindelar, P.T., Monda, L.E., & O'Shea, L.J. (1990). Effects of repeated readings on instructional- and mastery-level readers. *Journal of Educational Research, 83*, 220–226.

Stanovich, K.E. (1986). Matthew effects in reading: Some consequences of individual differences in the acquisition of literacy. *Reading Research Quarterly, 21*, 360–406.

Stauffer, R.G. (1980). *The language-experience approach to the teaching of reading* (2nd ed.). New York: Harper & Row.

Strickland, D.S. (1993). Some tips for using big books. In M.W. Olson & S.P. Homan, (Eds.). *Teacher to Teacher: strategies for the elementary classroom* (pp. 31–33). Newark, DE: International Reading Association.

Strickland, D.S., Ganske, K., & Monroe, J.K. (2002). *Supporting struggling readers and writers: Strategies for classroom intervention 3–6*. Newark, DE: International Reading Association.

Teale, W.H., & Shanahan, T. (2001). Ignoring the essential: Myths about fluency. *Illinois Reading Council Journal, 29*(3), 5–8.

Topping, K. (1987a). Paired reading: A powerful technique for parent use. *The Reading Teacher, 40*, 608–614.

Topping, K. (1987b). Peer tutored paired reading: Outcome data from ten projects. *Educational Psychology, 7*, 604–614.

Topping, K. (1989). Peer tutoring and paired reading: Combining two powerful techniques. *The Reading Teacher, 42*, 488–494.

Worthy, J., & Broaddus, K. (2001/2002). Fluency beyond the primary grades: From group performance to silent, independent reading. *The Reading Teacher, 55*, 334–343.

Young, T.A., & Vardell, S. (1993). Weaving readers theatre and nonfiction into the curriculum. *The Reading Teacher, 46*, 396–406.

Index

A

Accuracy, fluency and, 3
Anticipation Guide, 2
    answers, 75
Antiphonal Reading, 33
Appropriate expression, 3
Appropriate materials, 17, 20
Assessment methods, 7–13
    Classroom Fluency Snapshot,
        8–13
    5-Point Fluency Scale, 9
Assisted reading, 48–64

B

Basic sight words, 23–26

C

Choral Reading, 32
Classroom Fluency Snapshot, 8–13
Classroom instruction, 22–47
Comprehension, fluency and, 3, 17

D

Dolch list, revised, 25

E

Echo Reading, 31
Effect size, 15–16
Evidence-based strategies, activities,
    and resources, 19–71

F

5-Point Fluency Scale, 8, 9
Fluency
    accuracy and, 3
    appropriate expression and, 3
    appropriate materials and, 17, 20
    assessment methods for, 5–13
    comprehension and, 3, 16
    definition of, 3
    factors affecting, 17
    importance of, 3–4
    modeling of, 16, 17, 20
    practice and, 17

in silent reading, 4
    speed and, 3
Fluency Development Lesson, 42
Fluency instruction
    effect size and, 15
    evidence-based methods in, 19–71
    impact of, 14–15
    instructional time for, 14–15
    introduction of, 16
    principles of, 16–17
    research findings on, 15–16
Fluency research, 15–16
Function words, 23–24

G

Grade level, oral reading rates for,
    5–7

H

High-frequency words, 23–24, 26

I

Independent practice, 65–71
Independent reading, 21
Instructional materials, selection of,
    17, 20

L

Language Experience, 27–28

M

Matthew effects, 66
Meaning construction, 17
Modeling, 15–16, 17, 20

N

Neurological Impress Method, 52,
    61
Nouns, high-frequency, 26

O

Oral reading
    meaningful, 10, 14
    rates of, 3–7

round robin, 10, 14
    by teacher, 16, 17, 20
Oral Recitation Lesson, 40

P

Paired Reading, 49–51
Pattern books, 24
Peer tutoring, 53–55
Phrase boundaries, 47
Preview-Pause-Prompt-Praise,
    53–55

R

Radio Reading, 37–39
Read and Relax, 69–70
Readers Theater, 35–36
    The Grasshopper and the Ants,
        78–80
    Moira's Birthday, 81–85
Reading
    oral. See Oral reading
    sustained silent, 4, 21, 66–68
Reading fluency. See Fluency
Reading materials, selection of, 17,
    20
Reading Progress Chart
    for Reading While Listening, 64
    for Structured Repeated
        Readings, 56, 57, 58
Reading rates
    calculation of, 4–5
    fluency and, 3
    grade level–appropriate, 5–7
Reading While Listening, 61–64
Repeated Readings, 61
Research findings, 15–16
Revised Dolch list, 25
Round robin oral reading, 10, 14

S

Say It Like the Character, 43–44
Scripts for Readers Theatre
    The Grasshopper and the Ants,
        78–80
    Moira's Birthday, 81–85
Shared Book Experience, 29–30

Sight words, 23–24

Speed. *See* Reading rates

Stories, language experience, 27–28

Story map, 40, 41

Structured Repeated Readings, 7, 56–58

Super Signals, 45–46

Sustained silent reading, 21, 66–68
fluency in, 4

T

Tape, Check, Chart, 59–60

Teacher, oral reading by, 15, 17, 20

Tutoring, peer, Preview-Pause-Prompt-Praise technique in, 53–55

W

Word recognition
accuracy of, 16

Words correct per minute norms, 6–7

Words per minute norms, 5